Business
for Aspies

PORTLAND
PUBLIC LIBRARY

ENRICHING OUR COMMUNITY,
EXPANDING OUR WORLD.

First published in 2011
by Jessica Kingsley Publishers
116 Pentonville Road
London N1 9JB, UK
and
400 Market Street, Suite 400
Philadelphia, PA 19106, USA

www.jkp.com

Library of Congress Cataloging in Publication Data
A CIP catalog record for this book is available from the Library of Congress

British Library Cataloguing in Publication Data
A CIP catalogue record for this book is available from the British Library

ISBN 978 1 84905 845 2

Printed and bound in the United States by
Thomson-Shore, 7300 Joy Road, Dexter, MI 48130

To Rebekah Vaisey, one of the most beautiful, vibrant tangles of aliveness I have ever met. *Let your freak flag fly!*

And to the editor, Claire, at Jessica Kingsley Publishers who, with gentle encouragement, helped me cross the finish line.

Preface

I own and run a computer company in Silicon Valley, California. I work extensively with people who are on the spectrum in the technology sector. It saddens me every time I see someone brilliant relegated to a less challenging task due to misperceptions about ability. Since I have never been one to settle for the status quo, I have spent the last eight years searching for consistent, helpful, respectful methods of creating success for those with Asperger Syndrome (AS).

This book explores typical characteristics that define AS elaborating on each aspect while showcasing 42 different ways that your AS traits can make you an even better employee or boss. There are many traits such as "failure to develop peer relationships" that, according to diagnostic criteria, are impairments, yet, in the workplace, when properly recognized and properly positioned, can, as in this example, make you a focused, undeviating, project-driven employee; that is, the most valuable employee on the team.

In my work, I travel extensively and I am always seeking new talent for my little company and to figure out where to set up our next office. The more people I meet, the more I realize that people with AS have undiscovered, unappreciated talents that can be easily overlooked in the workplace. With the toughest problems, I often turn to someone with AS because I know they can focus clearly. With the most difficult, potentially emotionally volatile problems, I often turn to someone with AS because I know they have the wherewithal to stick to the facts.

As with many books, the main theory behind this work came from a well-studied expert. This theory was generated while sitting

Introduction

It is my personal belief that people with AS are often underestimated, underpaid, and have an untold amount of hidden potential. More than once, this realization has caused me deep sadness. It is sad to see anyone have their life force, their ability, their potential cut off, unexpressed, unnoticed, and unappreciated.

The work you do day in and day out should be enjoyable, perhaps hard, but always rewarding. Your job will probably take up the majority of hours in your waking life. At a typical job in the US, you might spend an hour in the morning getting ready for work, eight or nine hours at work, an hour commuting, and a few hours at night relaxing from work, trying to unwind from the stresses of the day. By simple logic, if you don't like your job, you probably don't like your life.

To put this concept into perspective in the most logical, hard-facts way, consider the calculation of total hours worked in a possible lifetime. The Centers for Disease Control and Prevention lists the US mortality rate at 78 years. Consider that you began work by the age of 20 (possibly doing some part-time work as a teenager, perhaps working part-time through college), retiring at 65. During your 45 years of employment, you work approximately 240 days a year, eight to nine hours a day. That's a grand total of 86,400–97,200 hours. With a little overtime, you could easily work 100,000 hours in your lifetime.

Your ability to build a career that brings you happiness is the one most important focus in any adult life. In my own experience I have met very few people with AS who are well-matched to their job. They often have unique, extreme talents that are either will redirect the question to me and I can answer it. Pretend you are a mirror reflecting the sun towards me. Do not talk. It's OK."

Michael's body relaxed enough so that he was able to walk into the building, shake hands, and sit down at the table, but he still looked sick. During the greeting and handshake, the executives tried small talk. I engaged in the conversation while Michael acted deaf. His behavior was odd, but still in the range of acceptable.

We sat down at the table and the executives introduced themselves. They all appeared to be techies with interests similar to my husband's interests. They were highly social business men savvy in the art of negotiation. They were not autistic—none showed traits of AS—but they shared a common love of computers with my husband.

Several minutes into the meeting the most bizarre thing happened.

After hearing enough technical information to catch his attention, my husband Michael *looked* at the executives as if they were real people. He could *see* them. He was open to them. His blinders fell away. Michael was silent, but I could see the fear melting. As I conversed with the executives I felt a small part of my mind trying to recall the last time Michael had looked at someone this openly when first meeting them. Perhaps he had done this before and I had not witnessed it? All I knew was that I could not recall a single time Michael had been able to engage in normal-esque eye contact when meeting someone for the first time.

I noticed the executives were looking too much to my husband for feedback. They sensed he was the technical one. Michael was giving only nods at this point, but I could see expectations building in the executives' approach.

I knew my husband was capable of giving eye contact in some situations, but I doubted that he could maintain it and I doubted that he could grasp the intricacies of fully reciprocal facial expressions, body gestures, and reparative language "tricks" used during intricate business negotiations. I started to worry that he might actually try being a part of the conversation.

Then it snowballed. My husband started answering questions, all technical, all needing more than a yes or no answer. He was engaged, fully engaged.

I sat in stunned silence through most of the remainder of the meeting. There were a few business-related questions that Michael sent my way but the meeting was quite obviously being led by Michael. He was leading people! He was in the position of shaping the conversation and he did a masterful job. He redirected; he gave thoughtful feedback; he reciprocated appropriately. He smiled, he nodded, he expressed agreement. These were conversational skills that I thought he would never understand let alone be able to do without rehearsed scripting. In this setting he looked and acted like my friends who had business degrees, MBAs with serious business training and social acumen.

When we left the meeting, I was the one shaking, not him. I was so happy. I had just witnessed a powerful ability in my husband. I have known my husband since he was 21 years old, and here he was at 41, navigating a highly complex social, professional interaction successfully.

What had happened?

First, I underestimated his abilities—I saw his inability to communicate and assumed that it covered all scenarios.

Second, both of us had failed to recognize that, in a certain environment, physical and social factors could combine to form a healthy, enjoyable social interaction for him.

Third, he had been physically prepared enough for the meeting.

These were simple solutions. Why had we not recognized them sooner? Stumbling upon this particular skill seemed so random. What if we had never discovered this ability? What if he had never known how amazing he could be?

The degree to which I had underestimated his abilities was shocking. I looked at other areas of my life, and I looked at other people I work with who experience varying shades of autism, and I found that there were many, many spikes in ability. I also found, to my dismay, that I regularly underestimated the abilities with an employer who will, it is hoped, see your contribution and help you grow long-term.

It is never too late. Even if you are 101 years old and this is the last thing you read before you die, it is not too late to shift your perception. It is especially important to do this if you are in the later years of your life. Take as much time as you can to relish the worth of your Aspie skills. Employment is really just a symbol of the world's appreciation of your talents. It is appreciation with a paycheck. But even if the world is not rewarding you monetarily, it is very helpful if you can, in your own mind, embrace your full self, twitches and all, and recognize that you are valuable. As you read this book, you will see the many ways you can turn your deficits into benefits.

The medical diagnosis for any condition shows you one side of the coin—the impairment, the disability, the difficulties. Let's explore the other side of the coin—the strengths, talents, and unmatched performance that a person with AS can achieve when in the right environment and when claiming his personality, his AS, as his own.

To back up my point, I will quote a recent business book titled, *Clever: Leading Your Smartest, Most Creative People* (Goffee and Jones 2009).

> Leaders realized that certain of their followers generated huge amounts of value for their organization. Their most valuable people were crucial to the success of the organization—and yet, at the same time, they were the most difficult to lead... They are individuals who make a disproportionate contribution to what the organization does. They habitually hit above their weight. ...the clever people we are talking about are capable of great things but only if the organizational and leadership context enables them to realize their potential. (p.x)

The world has been changed again and again by people such as yourself who walk outside the normal life path. Nurture your strengths.

CHAPTER 2

Executive Function

According to the Encyclopedia of Mental Disorders:

> The term executive function describes a set of cognitive abilities that control and regulate other abilities and behaviors. Executive functions are necessary for goal-directed behavior. They include the ability to initiate and stop actions, to monitor and change behavior as needed, and to plan future behavior when faced with novel tasks and situations. Executive functions allow us to anticipate outcomes and adapt to changing situations. The ability to form concepts and think abstractly are often considered components of executive function. (2010)

It is a well-known fact that executive function is not a forte for those with AS. You may have difficulties with project completion, scheduling, remembering various types of information, organization, and some tasks that may seem basic according to the general rules of "normal" development. That is OK.

A few examples to give you context: Roy's boss is often frustrated when Roy "plays dumb." Roy looks for a file in the file cabinet and he cannot find it. Roy has to ask for help and it appears like he is wasting other people's time.

If Roy could recognize that certain organizational tasks may never be easy enough for him, he could work around the frustration. In the situation of the difficult filing cabinet, he could work to find solutions. Depending on Roy's job description, there is a chance that the "file paper work" task can be given to someone else. There is also a chance he could keep his own separate small file drawer,

Now You See It; Now You Don't

My favorite solution to living with people who have strengths in areas other than executive function is to organize the living environment in a way where everything they need is visible and everything they do not need is hidden.

For example, at home the TV remote, wireless keyboard, and mouse (that go with the TV) are all set in front of the TV. They are not in a drawer. The dishes for dinner, which I hope they wash and use, are on a nice shelf with no doors. (Even a door with a glass front was a barrier.) Whenever we move to a new home, one of the first things I do is take the doors off the closets so that 1. my husband and children change their clothes regularly, and 2. the clothes are stored in the closet rather than on the floor outside the closet.

There are solutions, workable solutions, and, if done with good intent, they can bring you satisfaction in either making your own environment more enjoyable or in seeing someone with AS thrive, finding what they need easily and quickly.

In the work environment, you can do the same thing:

- Keep file folders in an open bin, not in a file cabinet.

- Keep an Inbox/Outbox for papers in the most exposed, thin-frame paper sorter you possibly can.

- Keep a pen and pencil cup on your desk, not in a drawer.

There is absolutely no reason to make your life any more difficult than it needs to be. The path to personal success often follows this standard procedure:

1. Identify problem.

2. Solve problem.

3. Forget the problem (leaving solution intact).

Many people skip that last step. They identify the problem, solve the problem, then remember the problem, complaining about it, remembering it as a problem they used to have. But, once it has been solved, it serves no purpose to give it any more attention.

In general, the goal is to keep the objects in your office to a bare minimum. Since you will need to keep things out when others are able to hide their stuff in drawers and cabinets, you will need to simply have less stuff. It may not seem fair, but if it solves the problem and you are able to work efficiently, then congratulations.

Organization of Events

While it is not always the case, people with low executive function have a hard time organizing the events of their lives. Upcoming meetings may be forgotten and important events often may be a surprise even though they were planned in advance. Anticipating events, planning for them, and organizing your schedule around them may not be a natural skill for you.

There are many, many organizational tools you can use, but most of these tools were designed by people with such strong executive function that they could spend their entire lives planning, planning, planning and be thrilled at seeing the plans through. As such, these tools are best used by people who also enjoy the act of planning.

If you try a few tools and they do not work for you, do not worry. There is a good chance the tool was developed for someone with a different mindset than yours. That is not bad. It is just different.

Several years ago author David Allen published a methodology called, *Getting Things Done* (Allen 2003). When Allen's book was first published, the tech sector embraced it and began using the strategies as standard protocol. Perhaps it was because the strategies are clearly delineated. Perhaps it was the purely logical, practical approach that appealed to a population with a high prevalence of AS. Perhaps it was the strong visual images David Allen used when describing his concepts. For many reasons, the organizational methods became popular in the tech sector, a field with a prevalence of people with AS.

Getting Things Done, GTD, is a relatively complex management system that allows you to take care of the many, many tasks you

Love/Belonging—This is our need to be socially accepted, to be part of a cultural and societal group. We have a primal need to be loved. But first we must have:

Safety/Security—This is a sense of safety, both physical and psychological. When this level is not fulfilled, a person experiences panic and agitation. If you are missing what you need on this level, you have a sense of danger, exposure, and vulnerability. But before you can reach this basic level you should have:

Basic Needs—Water, food, sleep, warmth, exercise, air, and so forth. This is the most fundamental level. Without it, the upper levels are at risk of crumbling.

Within the work environment, you can be most effective when your basic needs are met. For example, if you are hungry and cold, it will be hard to think about the job you need to complete. Each need fulfilled makes the next level more secure.

While these levels are shown in a linear, top to bottom way, they do not necessarily come in order. For example, you could be at a job where all needs are met and you are currently at the top of the pyramid, achieving new feats of invention. But things change when a new boss is hired who threatens your sense of safety with your team of colleagues. Perhaps he mocks you and others openly during meetings or perhaps he is unwilling to make special accommodations that a previous boss had and you no longer have an environment that suits you.

When a fundamental level is not strong, it makes the upper levels far weaker. For example, perhaps a colleague has spread an unpleasant and untrue rumor about you. It diminishes the middle need in the list—you no longer feel like you have a safe position within a welcoming social group. It affects your work, your ability to concentrate, and you are no longer functioning at peak performance.

What would Maslow's pyramid look like when interpreted through the AS diagnostic criteria? Let's start from the bottom up to show the many steps you take to create a happy, fulfilling adult career:

Basic Needs—Issues with self-help skills can make it a bit more difficult to make this foundational level solid. For example, going to the employee break room for lunch might be enough sensory overload that it might make it hard for you to eat. You are hungry again by 2pm, but cannot take another break until 4pm. In the meantime the quality of your work suffers.

Sleep may be a little less comfortable if you have a hard time keeping a bedroom clean (executive function organizational skills). Exercise, which is actually on this foundational level, may be more difficult for someone with sensory issues. While the items on this level may be more difficult for someone with an AS brain and body, these needs are the most important, most basic, and most vital for your success as an adult.

Safety/Security—If you can achieve the basic need level, then you can focus on the safety level. For someone who may not be able to interpret body language and various communications from others, personal safety may not be easy. For example, if you are crossing the street in front of the office and cannot tell if someone is going to stop to let you cross or is going to run over you (perhaps the driver cannot see you), then most definitely your personal safety will be threatened in many situations. The simple baseline is that your safety is not guaranteed and it is not something you can necessarily improve. The key is to do everything you are able to build in as much safety as possible in as many areas as you can for as long as you can (see the next Best Practice for a few ideas).

Love/Belonging—This level may be either the hardest or the easiest for someone with AS. If you want to be an accepted, included part of the team, you will need to work harder than most to achieve this step. If you do not care much about what others think of you, then this area may be a bit easier for you. In fact, it may be even easier than if you were an NT; if you don't need or crave the social interactions that appear to be the norm in everyone else's lives, then you have less to worry about.

in your work environment or at least look like you are engaged, while maintaining a sense of safety. By "safety" we mean that you are not being pushed into overload.

This strategy is successful because it is based in Maslow's Hierarchy of Needs (outlined in a previous section). Maslow's theories were based on norms that are interpreted differently with an Aspie brain.

Previously I described the five levels then I gave a description of how those levels can be interpreted through the AS diagnostic criteria. Now let's look at the five levels of need and how they would manifest themselves at work, starting with the first most basic step, the bottom of the pyramid:

Basic Needs—These most basic physical needs at work will often be: a safe work environment (no dangerous materials), access to water, access to a restroom, the ability to move freely when needed, food when you need it.

If you have sensory issues, you may have requests for basic needs that are outside of the norm. For example, one of your basic needs may be "peace and quiet" which may be impossible in many work situations. The best solution for issues on this level is to, first, see if your employer, colleagues, or work environment can meet these needs. If not, find a work environment that can satisfy this most basic, most important level of need.

If you need a more quiet environment, try wearing headphones while working. If you need it dimmer, try dimming the lights near your desk. Something as simple as having a mostly black poster near your computer can dampen the light sufficiently. If physical touch is difficult, notify your colleagues and they should quickly learn the boundaries.

One super easy solution that seems to work: weights. There has been great research showing that wearing a weighted vest can calm an Aspie's sensory system. The classic weighted vest used in occupational therapy is not practical for the office, but a light jacket with coins or other weighty objects in the pockets works. A pair of pants with several heavy objects in the pockets works.

Heavier-than-normal fabric may even help. For example, a sturdy blue jeans jacket or blue shirt made out of similarly heavy material may provide you with a surprisingly helpful little edge in staying calm and focused at work.

Personally I have seen the weighted vests work wonders. I have seen many employees with heavy pockets, but the most drastic example I saw was with my own child, Stephen.

It was his second day at a new school and I was standing at the classroom door, waiting to pick up Stephen. The classroom teacher walked over to me and quietly said, "Stephen has been a bit spacey today." Poor little Stephen was staring off into space whispering something to himself, probably reciting pi, "3.14159265358979323846..."

I said his name and he did not hear me. So, I pressed both of his shoulders down for several seconds. His eyes opened wide; he looked over at me, then looked at the teacher and said, "Hi!"

I grinned at the teacher and said, "Just press the On button!"

Stephen giggled as only a preschooler can do and ran back to his desk. He noticed everyone was packing up for the day and he began packing his backpack too.

These seemingly meaningless little bits of sensory input are so easy to overlook and so powerful when applied. Using sensory input techniques may help "wake you up" enough to see the papers in front of you, plan for a deadline, or remember an important meeting.

Safety/Security—This is physical safety, economic security, freedom from threats, and even emotional safety. In a work environment physical safety needs should be met (at least in the US) by federal, state, and local requirements. In the US, each state has some type of Employment Development, Employee Rights, or a Department of Labor and Industry office that protects employees (and takes loads of taxes from employers!). In California, the Employment Development Department, www.edd.ca.gov makes sure that everyone in the state has their basic safety needs met. When certain needs are not met, new legislation is usually in process to make sure that those needs will soon be protected.

To find out if there are existing laws to help you attain the work environment that best fits your needs, search online for the name of your state, city, region, or country plus search terms such as:

- employee rights
- employee protection
- department of labor
- workplace fairness
- labor law.

Most often, you can find great solutions at work without having to mention your legal protections, but it does help to know what rights are already protected and which are not.

Loving/Belonging—In the work environment, this need is the most difficult and possibly the most avoidable. There is a chance that you can build security and success in your career while not engaging in social relations to the same degree as colleagues. There is a chance you can avoid a few of the meetings, avoid a few face-to-face interactions, and slowly ease this particular load.

For non-AS people this level of need may not in fact be a need at all.

The belonging level includes acceptance, being part of a group, and identification with a successful team. These things are nice, but may not be as fulfilling for you as for someone who is more socially extroverted. Part of the definition of "extrovert" is "life of the party." Unless that term has been used to describe you in the past, then this is an area where you may be able to relax.

Ego/Esteem—Ego and a sense of self are built when you are assigned to important projects and when you get recognition for those projects. Esteem refers to your status among peers, again something that may not rank quite so high on your list of needs.

Peak Experience—The top level is the level where people with AS shine the brightest. Peak experiences are:

- challenging experiences

- opportunities for innovation and creativity

- learning and creating at a high level.

A person with AS functioning on this level can do amazing things. This is where your hyper-focus comes into play, at the top of the Maslow-for-Aspies pyramid.

Living near the University of California at Berkeley, I see upfront every day how brilliant people with AS can be. For example, my two youngest children have a poster of the periodic table of elements on their ceiling so they can look at it as they go to sleep at night. Several of the synthetic elements were discovered at the university: berkelium, californium, and lawrencium are a few. They were all discovered by people who had a sufficiently satisfied level of safety (satisfied to their personal need) so they could devote themselves adequately to their work.

Perhaps the solutions to achieving that baseline of safety will be easier than you think, at least for achieving an environment of safety at work. For one man with AS, it was simple. At his desk he has:

1. A drawer full of "fidget toys," various things he can play with while thinking, including juggling balls and hacky sacks.

2. A Rubik's cube.

3. A picture of his wife. While their relationship is not politically correct, she takes care of most of his basic needs so that he can stay as healthy and focused as possible.

For others it may be a particular type of candy, a figurine of your favorite cartoon or movie character, or a special pillow you use on your seat or behind your back. Find what comforts you.

Once you have identified your successful basic safety strategies at work, try to find ways to return to safety after difficult situations.

or not. Keeping your distance helps keep relationships professional.

- One element of friendship is often secret-keeping. While most secrets are harmless, there are some that can seriously damage a company. Enron became the tsunamic disaster it did in part due to too many people keeping too many secrets. If there had been fewer buddies and more people with AS in the ranks, the disaster may have been averted sooner.

- Friends do not tattle on each other, but colleagues do. If someone on the team is doing something dishonest or wrong, it is far easier to tell management if you do not have to worry about harming a friendship.

- The closer you become as friends, the better you get to know their families and their intimate personal lives. It is much harder to work with someone if you know their private details. For example, many years ago my husband and I were invited to the house of a co-worker. The home was overrun with large dogs who had chewed large chunks off the furniture. Michael is extremely sensitive to visual input. Anything that appears "messy" to him can cause him to go into overload. As Michael stood at this co-worker's door, he could not enter the home. I saw what was happening and made a quick excuse for why we were just going to say hello and then "go take care of a family emergency." The family emergency was Michael's overload; it was true enough. While any major damage was curtailed, the initial damage of seeing this image of his co-worker did actually damage Michael's ability to work with this particular co-worker. Some social distance would have made it much easier in the long run for Michael to work with this co-worker.

CHAPTER 4

Eye Contact and Reading Faces at Work

The countenance is the portrait of the mind, the eyes are its informers.

—Cicero, De Oratore

I love seeing various expressions in a person's eyes. The thoughts going through another person's mind are so easily read in the way the eyes move (and of course the rest of the face).

In contrast, when my husband looks in my eyes, he sees "nothing", and when I look at his, they are generally expressionless also. The eyes are not a necessary method of communication, just a nice method for those who enjoy it.

That said, if you see "nothing" in a person's eyes, you may believe that you can skip this section. Please do not. The eyes are a powerful communication tool and, even without you intending to, you can fall into serious problems if an effort is not made to communicate successfully at work. Your eyes may appear "shifty," causing people to distrust you or perhaps blame you when things go wrong. You may be blamed for sexual harassment if you stare too long in the wrong location.

I hope those reasons will convince you to read on.

Best Practice 3: When Less Is More

When you have a hard time interpreting facial expressions, the first and easiest thing to do is to look more closely at the face for clues. Unfortunately for those with face-reading difficulties (either too much or too little information), staring is a natural way to get information.

People generally dislike staring.

If someone tells you to "stop staring" there are many ways you can accomplish this and still do what you need to do (study and learn).

1. Count. Look at the person's face and count to three. Glance away at the sky, the wall, the desk, whatever, then look again. One, two, three, glance away. You can glance away either while they are talking or while you are talking. Either is equally risky.

2. When the person looks away, take that opportunity to look at their face. When they look at you, wait one second, then look away also. It is a type of dance that alleviates some of the weight of a full eye-contact conversation.

3. Mimic their facial expressions. When they raise their eyebrows, raise yours slightly too. When they smile, smile too. It is a brilliant way to keep in sync with the person you are talking to. People with neurotypical brains do this without thinking about it. It actually creates a bond between the two people talking if they see the other person mirror their expressions.

   Be careful not to copy exactly. Mimic most of the expressions in a more mild, less "loud" way and you may find that your colleagues treat you more like a team-mate.

4. Plaster a gentle smile on your face. One woman with autism said, "I practiced this by pulling the corners of my mouth up and I held them there. Once I felt the facial muscle I could flex it any time I wanted." The one facial expression that is least likely to get you into trouble (when

you cannot read or respond to another person's expression) is the smile. A muted, gentle smile is a good idea. Not a big Cheshire cat smile that will draw attention to you, but a mild, calm, generally happy smile.

Warning: If you find yourself staring at someone who is talking to you, you may think that glancing at various parts of the face will "break up" the staring enough to make it less of a problem. Not so. When two people are feeling romantically attracted, one of the key "turn-ons" is glancing from one part of the face to another: from the cheeks, to lips, to the eyes... Apparently, this is how people find appropriate mates—by giving a full review of the person's bone structure, genetic traits, and so on.

This is definitely not something to do at work. Ever.

When studying a person's face for clues to the message they are communicating, try to either glance away between each observation of a different feature or try to view the whole face at once, not moving your own eyes, but taking mental note of what you are seeing.

In the end, know that eye contact is difficult. There are many aspects of eye-to-eye gaze as a form of communication that researchers are still discovering and we are only learning now. The future will bring us even more information about eye contact.

Best Practice 4: Relaxing
Your Eyes—Face Muting

If looking someone in the eye is overwhelming and no benefit will come from forcing yourself towards overload, then do not do it. You are an adult and you have free will.

If someone is punitive for lack of eye contact at this phase of life, it can be an abusive request. There are ways you can deal with overwhelming eye contact, but forcing yourself to plummet into overload should never be an option.

That said, it is a nice bonus to be able to look at someone's face without difficulty. People like it when you look at them. For some bizarre reason (a reason that does not make much sense to the AS brain) eye contact makes people feel trust, warmth, and good feelings. People are generally nicer to you when you give them appropriate eye contact. The benefits are often worth the effort.

So, how to do it so you do not feel like you are spinning out of control? One trick is to "mute" the face, minimizing the amount of input you get when in a situation where eye contact should be given. By minimizing input, you minimize the chance of overload.

A few potential solutions, starting with the most obvious and ending with the most effective, valuable solutions for the workplace, follow here:

Solution 1. Look near their eyes. Leo, my oldest son, looks at people's foreheads. He tried looking at people's eyebrows but "they look like caterpillars dancing and I often ended up smiling or laughing inappropriately." The forehead creases, raises, and lowers with various expressions, but it is generally a safe place.

Solution 2. Look at a part of their body that is actually blank. Judy looks at people's necks or collarbones. Note that it is important to never look lower than the neck in a workplace environment. Looking at the chest is an overt sexual gesture and could easily be construed as sexual harassment.

Solution 3. Glance away often as described in the previous Best Practice. This is my favorite advice because it builds tolerance. It makes it possible to increase your ability to look someone in the eye.

Solution 4. Do not look at all. Act distracted. Be "busy with something." If this is the best you can do, this is the best you can do. This is Daniel's favorite, currently working at a government lab alongside Nobel Laureates and brilliant scientists. This strategy works for him mostly because he has gotten very good at doing it well.

When you first try it you may run into problems. If the person asks "Are you listening?" you can reply, "I'm concentrating on what you are saying; I just need to get this done. Go on." Continue sorting papers or doing whatever it is you were doing with your hands while the person talks. Glance up occasionally, but, for the most part, do not bother looking as you keep your hands busy with something else.

Solution 5. Allow your eyes to glaze over. If you have not yet learned how to do this, it is a highly valuable skill to have. Through various sources of information (psychology texts, child development texts, etc.) you can learn that, when the eyes glaze over, the person is often thinking of something else. You may get comments such as "Are you listening?" if you do not use this technique well.

To learn how to glaze over your eyes, look at someone who does not care if you are looking at them. Now think of something you really enjoy thinking about. For myself, it would be a memory of a country I have traveled to for business. For my husband with AS it would be programming. He would think of a particular bug he is trying to fix and his eyes would see the code, reading line by line.

Once you know how to glaze over your eyes, seeing something other than what is in front of you, practice doing it while showing the physical posture and facial expression of someone who is listening. You can get very good at this with a little effort.

A description from Michael:

> I allow my eyes to relax. I don't see the person anymore, but I look at their face, well, it's not actually looking… I point my eyes towards them, nod every now and then, and if what they are saying is interesting, I listen a bit. I glance away from time to time so it doesn't look like staring. If I just want them to stop talking, I nod a bit, then say, "Oh I'm getting a phone call. Just a minute." I pull my phone out of my pocket, smile nicely at the person who was talking, and step away from the conversation. It's nice to know that I am never stuck talking to someone.

The fact is that most work conversations are actually not necessary. Neurotypical people often enjoy talking for the sake of talking, for that emotional connection they get when they communicate something to you. You have the luxury of not needing that connection.

The following epigraph explains why some neurotypicals may engage in conversation:

> *The happiest conversation is that of which nothing is distinctly remembered, but a general effect of pleasing impression.*
>
> —*Samuel Johnson*

Note that it is very important to determine first if the person is going to communicate something you need to be aware of. If it is something important, perhaps consider the next strategy—eye contact avoidance—since it will free up the mental space you need to process what the person is saying.

You may use eye contact avoidance:

1. When you know eye contact will overload you.

2. When the person who is talking to you has important information for you and you must give your full attention (and you can only give full attention by avoiding the eye contact).

3. When you just do not feel like it.

It is also a generally good idea to avoid eye contact from time to time. Not always, but sometimes (and in some work environments, avoid it often). It is a brilliant tactic for the workplace.

Why would it be "brilliant" to avoid eye contact from time to time? Because in nearly every workplace, bosses value efficient employees who are focused on getting their work done. The best way to gain professional success is by being and appearing to be an efficient, focused worker who is more dedicated to the task at hand than to chatting with people. While this is not the case in every work situation, it is a solid general rule. As an employer, I can vouch for the fact that I promote most quickly the employees who appear to be the most focused.

Consider Stewart's experience as an employee:

My bosses have always liked me and I think it's because I keep conversations to a minimum, even with the boss. I don't get distracted from my work by people trying to get my attention. If I don't look at them or reciprocate the conversation like they want, they shut up pretty fast. They think I'm a grump sometimes, but I make it up by doing good work that makes their jobs easier.

I even keep work-related conversations down to the bare minimum. People condense what they are saying when they know you are barely listening and if you are not giving eye contact then you are barely listening. All these conversations that people have at work are mostly a waste of time.

Stewart is given pay raises often and every employee review noted his dedication. This has been in large part due to his avoidance of eye contact! What a benefit!

Asperger Syndrome has benefits that can translate well to highly paid, highly rewarding professional careers.

A word of caution

Note that, to succeed in some careers, eye contact, chatting in the hallway, and "hobnobbing it" with colleagues is what gets you pay raises. Perhaps these particular workplaces are not a great fit for someone who has skills in other areas.

Another potential aspect of eye contact avoidance that will help you avoid problems—when you do avoid eye contact, do it in a confident way, with your shoulders straight and the rest of your body relaxed. If you avoid eye contact in a suspicious way (shoulders hunched, tight muscles, panicky facial expression) then avoiding the eye contact will cause you more problems than if you had made the effort in the first place. When you do wish to avoid eye contact, make sure your body is calm and confident so the eye contact avoidance is interpreted simply as you being preoccupied with a work-related task.

For some people with AS, the face is an overwhelming map of movement and position that makes little sense. For others, the face is blank. (In the middle is the neurotypical, easy understanding of facial expressions.) We just reviewed what to do when the face is overwhelming. Now let's look at what to do if the face gives you no information or insufficient information.

Best Practice 5: Training Your Eyes—Mapping the Blank Face

What if all you see is a blank face? When I ask my husband "Look at my face. What do you see?" his reply is usually, "Nothing."

There are two documented medical conditions that interfere with a person's ability to read faces. First, is *prosopagnosia*, otherwise known as faceblindness. It is usually caused by acute brain damage, but researchers are starting to uncover that it can also be congenital. It affects approximately 2.5 percent of the population.

With faceblindness, the part of the brain that differentiates between various facial features is nonfunctional. A person with full faceblindness will not be able to identify the age, race, or other details of a person's facial identity. A person with faceblindness will depend on cues such as clothes, hair, voice, or other details to identify people—both strangers and people they see every day.

Casey, a young man with AS, had a rough start when he started his first job. He alienated several people who could have been of great assistance to him at work. On the third day of work, Casey's trainer asked him "Why are you acting odd…like you're meeting me for the first time?" Casey, who at this time did not know about faceblindness, blamed his own stupidity, thinking he was inattentive and careless rather than faceblind.

There is a similar type of blindness called mindblindness, discovered by Simon Baron-Cohen. Mindblindness is commonly defined as an inability to recognize that another person has a mind separate from your own. This causes the mindblind person to have extreme difficulty guessing which response to give in social communication

Whether due to faceblindness, mindblindness, or just a simple weakness in identifying facial expressions, the part of the brain that assists with these perceptions is simply not activated in many people with AS. It is not a fault per se—there are other skills that are activated with AS that are not activated for most people. It is a trade-off. Unless it causes insurmountable difficulties at work, perhaps it would be helpful to follow the classic three steps:

1. Recognize it.

2. Either find solutions or accept it.

3. Get on with your work.

If you wish to "accept it" and "get on with your work," then you may want to use the following phrases with the people you work with:

> "I am sorry, but I do not read faces as well as most people do. Can you be more clear with the words you are using?"

> or

> "Thanks for explaining this, but I hear words a lot more than I hear other cues. Can you be very direct with your words so I can fully understand what you are saying?"

> or

> "I am not sure what you are saying, but I can tell there is something I am missing. Can you be very direct in how you are saying it?"

If you wish to figure out how to read the facial expressions, take confidence in the fact that many resources are being built to help us all, AS or not, read faces, which in turn helps us read minds. The more we can understand what is in a person's mind, the more we can understand what we need to do at work.

Currently, new ground is being broken by the Facial Action Coding System, FACS, developed by Paul Ekman (Ekman and Rosenberg 2005). This is a clinical way to read facial expressions, a skill that is critical for most in-person communications. The book is fairly expensive, but you can learn quite a lot by searching http:// face-and-emotion.com and other sites that help us understand facial expressions.

When you learn it by rote, you will have a far better understanding of *exactly* what a person means, but may miss the messages that occur when a person is conflicted; that is, when a person says one thing, but means another. For example, a person may be showing a facial expression of frustration, but be talking about someone they supposedly like at work. Seeing the contrast between the accurate emotion through the facial expression as it directly disagrees with the words may be confusing. People are complex.

One tell-tale sign of AS is eye avoidance. In one of my sons, the eye avoidance was obvious since infancy. His first pediatrician said, "I've never seen an infant struggle like this to not look at his mother...or at me." While eye avoidance may appear from birth, I believe that eye avoidance can develop as a survival strategy in difficult environments. Used often enough, it becomes a habit.

In my experience, my husband with AS has the potential of recognizing the full intensity of a person's face, but the facial recognition part of his brain has numbed itself purposefully.

When Michael is relaxed and calm, he comments that a person's facial expressions are "distracting." The face could not "distract" if it was blank. The safer he feels, the more often I hear him comment about expressions.

Yet, when someone is angry, his ability to read a face completely disappears. The face becomes a complete blank. My best guess is that he has a brain prone to faceblindness and, due to early environmental trauma, this part of his brain shuts down as a self-protective measure.

When he was a boy, one forceful adult in his life often grabbed him by the chin saying, "Look me in the eye when I am talking to you." Grabbing a person's chin is an aggressive, dominant, controlling act. The jaw is a critical joint and, in the moment of domination, it strips the person of free will. Doing it to a little person is particularly harmful. As a little boy he could not escape. He could not look away. He could close his eyes, but that made the person more angry, so he learned not to do that either. Instead, his survival instinct kicked in and he obeyed, doing the only thing left to him—going numb.

In this situation, his brain, his wonderful, brilliant autistic brain, protected itself by shutting down the overload. Perhaps the brain blocked the intensely angry information it saw on the face the same way people block memories of war, trauma, or any other difficult experience.

When we were newlyweds, I once touched my husband's chin in a loving gesture. He had the first fit of rage I had ever seen. It was terrifying to see the pain that was buried in his sensory system. He lashed out like a caged animal. He punched a hole in the wall. The "chin grab" triggered intense anger. He was an adult now and no one was going to force him to "look me in the eye" again. The physiological reaction was so intense it completely overwhelmed his ability to think rationally. I have not touched him on the chin since.

I doubt my husband's experience is unique. In 2007, when the book *Look Me in the Eye: My Life with Asperger's* by John Elder Robison was released, both Michael and I laughed. We had considered his sensitivity to be a unique situation, but apparently there were others with AS who had experienced the same.

Whether Michael's faceblindness existed since birth or the ability was shut down purposefully, there is a possibility you can train this important part of your brain to read faces clinically through basic studies of the Facial Action Coding System.

If you are faceblind and have a very difficult time learning to read faces, perhaps consider yourself lucky. When you see nothing on a person's face it is actually easier than when a person's face is overwhelming. It is easier because:

1. There is more to conversation than just the facial expression.

fixes that need to be done. She is able to stay in her comfortable home environment where things are organized exactly as she likes them.

In the first few years of working for the company, Sarah was asked to come in for staff meetings. The anticipation of the meeting made her sick for days. She called in sick to the first meeting and was so late to the second meeting that she was sure she would be fired. After that meeting, she emailed her boss, explaining that she loved her job and meetings were tough for her to attend. She offered to work several extra hours completing a side project that no one else wanted to do. She offered it as compensation for the missed staff meetings. Her boss saw the benefit for him and agreed heartily.

(If you do not have eye contact aversion but want to understand the difficulty, read the book *Look Me in the Eye* by John Elder Robison (2009). It gives a lifelong view of how a person with eye contact aversion struggled with various jobs.)

Bottomline: Jobs that have less face-time are often more flexible.

When you work in an office, people can see what you do. If you get a horrible email from your boss, you cannot have a meltdown. You have to hold yourself together. If you experience sensory overload, you cannot stim to calm yourself down.

Even if you have your own office with a door and no window letting people in the hallway see you, there is still the constant possibility of people stopping by your office to ask random questions, interrupting your work, and creating mental havoc in your routine. For years my husband had an office with a door and no visual access from the hallway. Despite this privacy, he was still on alert for the eight, ten, sometimes twelve hours at work every day. That is a long time to be actively trying to be normal every day. He would consciously try to shift his schedule to work after everyone else was gone so that he could have at least some time at the office when he was not "on alert."

You have far more flexibility when you work from home. (This is true only if you have a calm, quiet home environment that you can modify to fit your needs.)

If you can manage to find a career that allows you to work from home or in a fully private environment then this entire section of the diagnosis can be ignored, at least for career purposes.

If you believe you would work best with 0 percent face-time, first ask yourself:

1. Do you have the space available at home or elsewhere that you could use as a comfortable office space? Would you be able to focus effectively on your work there? (Discussed in a previous section on executive function.)

2. Do you have the ability to work on something from start to finish without someone keeping you on track? (Also discussed in the section on executive function.)

3. Do you know where to find a job that will work for you? (Discussed below.)

Telecommuting became a fad in the 1980s and 1990s, but in the 2000s it was a cost-cutting measure and now in the 2010s it has become a common solution for all parties involved: the employer, the employee, and the environment that is impacted by commuters.

Working from a remote office (telecommuting) has become accepted on a wide enough scale that there are many "virtual companies" that employ only telecommuting employees. When meetings are needed, they pick a country and have the meeting there. One example is the open source software company Canonical. All employees work from home (or wherever they wish) so company meetings are held in Prague, Barcelona, Seville, Brussels, and Dallas, Texas to name a few. Having only occasional meetings can be a cost-effective and enjoyable way to run a company.

Many telecommuting jobs are available for those willing to do what it takes to get them. A few resources:

• **www.guru.com** is a resource I use for my company. When I need someone to do a brochure for a conference, I post a job on www.guru.com and within a few hours I have a bid from someone who is probably working from home in their pajamas. The work gets done, money is exchanged, and everyone is happy.

- **www.elance.com** is also a reputable site for finding gainful employment that allows you the freedom to work without the typical social encumbrances of an office job.

Both www.guru.com and www.elance.com are international—it does not matter where you live if you want to work or hire work. Other resources in the US are the following:

- **www.craigslist.org** often has jobs that are geared towards unique schedules and unique arrangements. Remember to check craigslists in areas other than where you live. For example, if you live in a little town in Idaho, your cost of living is inexpensive, especially rent or mortgage. But if you look for a telecommuting job in the San Francisco or Los Angeles area where the cost of living is quite high, you may be able to find a better salary than if you had looked only within your area.

- **www.monster.com**, **www.dice.com**, or other job search engines may be able to save you time by instantly eliminating all jobs that require in-office face-time. Monster does not currently have a telecommuting filter, but Dice allows you to select "Search Telecommuting Jobs Only" in the Advanced Search area.

Best Practice 7: Building Skills for Ultimate Flexibility—Removing the Pressure for In-Person Work

How do you build the skills you need to do telecommuting jobs? Nearly all the skills can be learned by accessing resources online. Self-taught experts are often the most competent and skilled workers. They obviously have the motivation to figure things out on their own. (That said, there are some jobs, such as lawyers and professors, that do require an advanced degree.)

Before you are discouraged about not being able to self-teach the skills for a high-end professional job, please read the following story of a personal friend. He is a clear example of how you can build a career regardless of your circumstance or limitations.

Matt grew up in a difficult home. His father was often violent. His mother was often on drugs. When Matt was 14 years old, he managed to get a judge to grant him emancipation. To do this, a different adult had to claim responsibility for Matt. Matt's friend's father filled in and for a short time Matt was safe.

Matt was not able to sustain the relationship with his friend and Matt soon lost his court-ordered "parent." Matt was now homeless, family-less, and on the street. He was a "good kid" who was struggling through a tough life.

For a while, Matt lived at the library during open hours, got food from the school's garbage bins, and slept in a hidden corner behind the school building at night. But one night a guard found him and Matt was expelled from school. Matt tried to explain his situation, but the school staff could not see past his social awkwardness. His lack of ability to communicate his situation clearly looked suspicious in their eyes. As with many people with AS, Matt's inability to say the right things caused people to misjudge him.

Now at 15 years old, Matt was not only homeless and family-less, but now school-less, completely without support.

At this crucial turning point in his life, at a time when Matt could have been completely overcome with self-hatred for his inability to show people that he was a good kid, instead he turned his focus towards building a successful career.

Matt spent one week studying various technical skills on the computers at the local library. Matt created a resume for himself listing skills that he knew he could develop quickly. Matt submitted his resume to several local tech firms, all within walking distance because he did not even own a bicycle.

Since Matt was tall for his age and already had facial hair coming in, it was relatively easy for him to give the impression of a geeky university-educated young man, significantly older than he actually was.

Matt worked and studied 18, sometimes 19, hours a day to figure out how to do what he had been hired to do. Matt slept a few blocks away from work. In his words, "Five or six hours of sleep is plenty when you have to hide where no dogs, police, or passers-by will find you."

After receiving his first paycheck, Matt was able to begin looking for a room to rent. Matt was officially launched into the adult world of work at the tender age of 15.

The time that Matt spent as an office worker was difficult for him, but since he was always moving from one computer problem to the next, providing technical support for the entire office, no one person at the office was able to notice his anomalies to a significant enough degree for it to have a negative impact on Matt's work.

Matt progressed from one job to the next, slowly developing the talents and skills needed to work independently from a home office. Now that Matt is in his own personal home office, he finally feels the peace and self respect he has always craved.

Matt's story is an extreme example, and I hope, dear reader, that you have not had a similar experience. The severity of Matt's experience showcases well how a person can build a brilliant career by focusing on what he *can* do and not focusing on the obstacles.

If Matt had focused on the obstacles, it is highly likely that he would have stayed on the streets. His life would have undoubtedly followed a much less fortunate path.

The field that allows you the easiest entrance to build highly valuable skills is the field of Linux development. You can "work" as a writer, programmer, designer, bug fixer, or even just someone who uses the software and finds the bugs. When you work on a piece of software, you volunteer your time and do whatever you can, whenever you can. You work alongside many other volunteers. You can put it on your resume as past experience. If your volunteer team completes a full project, you can list that as an accomplishment. Employers like myself often look to the Linux field to find people who are already obviously passionate about building their talents.

A quick background on how the Linux field works: In the early 90s, Linus Torvalds, a Finnish man living in Sweden, began writing a kernel. A kernel is the code that is at the center, at the start, of an operating system. An operating system is the thing that makes your computer work. There are three main operating systems generally referred to as: Apple, Windows, and Linux.

A little more background so you can see the field as a whole: In the 80s, Bill Gates, still at college at Harvard, began by writing a BASIC interpreter. At one point, he managed to get a meeting with IBM. IBM asked Bill Gates to write an operating system for them. Bill said he could do it, so he went to the Seattle Users' Group (a group of volunteers who write code for the fun of writing code) and Bill purchased DOS from the group.

In 1984 Steve Jobs and Steve Wozniack launched the first computers using the Macintosh operating system. In response, Bill Gates wrote Windows (an operating system originally based on DOS). In 1991 Linus first posted on a message board that launched Linux development into the world at large.

Out of the four men directing the building of these operating systems, three exhibited mild to moderate autistic traits (all but Steve Jobs). They were all developing competing operating systems in tandem.

Why include all this explanation? Because only one of these fields allows people with AS to enter at their choice, at their leisure, and on their own terms. There are probably more people with autism thriving in Linux development than in any other area of the technical sector. It is perhaps surprising that the Linux community is one of the most supportive, socially active communities online.

There is one crucial difference between the three types of computer. Each operating system has a unique philosophy behind it. It is important to know what these are so you can see why the Linux field is open to you:

1. Apple was built by Steve Jobs and Steve Wozniack. Wozniack, often called Woz, was the techie. According to my contacts who have worked with Wozniack, he is "comfortably geeky." That said, Woz left Apple in its early days and now the company is directed by Jobs, someone who believes in keeping tight control on product development. This means that you must actually be hired by Apple to develop software for their computers.

freely. It was a virtual effort—no office, no main location, no physical location. There have been many different variations and split-offs, called "forks." Today there are many strong operating systems, Ubuntu, Fedora, Red Hat, Mint, etc., that are referred to colloquially as Linux. Linus Torvalds and Eric Raymond now co-manage the Linux kernel (the starting point of the operating system).

Note that there were many, many other contributors along the way, some of whom would probably be offended by my severe over-simplification of how this type of software is developed, but my purpose in explaining the development of free and open software is solely to open up this field for readers who may be seeking a way into a field that grants them personal and professional freedom. Linux is currently the most common, well-known term so it is the term used.

The Linux operating system is maintained mostly by volunteers but some companies such as Red Hat and Canonical (Ubuntu) have sprouted up, starting successful businesses building off free and open Linux software. Red Hat does not allow volunteers to contribute to their work, but Canonical does. Canonical goes to extreme measures to make sure that anyone, anywhere can contribute. They welcome new contributors with open arms. Many software projects are looking for volunteers to help them grow. You simply go online and look for projects you may enjoy contributing to. Search for:

- Contribute to Linux
- Volunteer, Linux
- Google Code
- SourceForge
- Launchpad.

In general, the other people on the boards are accustomed to answering questions so do not be afraid to ask. First, do everything you can to figure it out yourself, then just ask.

There is a chance that while you were reading this section you became discouraged by a personal lack of technical knowledge. Great news. You do not need to be technically savvy in order to work in the tech industry. There are many things you can do besides program. You can:

- find bugs

- edit documentation

- suggest new features for the software

- create graphics for the project

- help with a website for the project

- maintain a FAQ of How To documentation

- tell people about the project or write articles for publication

- send a letter or email of appreciation to the programmers

- test the program

- work on many more tasks that are appropriate to the particular project on which you are working.

This is only a small list of potential tasks. There is surely a task that fits your particular skill set. Please do not think that the tech world and other high-level professions are only for the ultra-brilliant. Trust me, they are not. These fields are full of people like you and I, people with large chunks of disability, fault, and ineptitude. For example, I have one particular fault that puts me at a serious disadvantage when compared to others. I experienced an illness in my late 20s that wiped out chunks of my memory. Certain things that should be obvious often have me stumped, completely clueless, and unable to connect the dots in seemingly simple conversations. It is embarrassing. It is socially painful. But for years I have forced this disability to be as small as possible. I make mistakes and move on.

I have a choice: I can focus on this disability and let it limit my career choices or I can push past it and refocus on my better traits. By nearly all measures I have been successful. There is nothing significant that I would change about my current career (except for a higher salary, which is probably a common desire for nearly everyone!). I have a stable career that allows me the freedom I crave at this point in my life. Since I built a life as CEO, I get to hire and fire while I build a work force that works well together. I get to create an office that I enjoy coming to every day. I am fully confident that, if I had focused on my weaknesses, I would never have ventured into the tech sector.

My previous stereotype was that the tech sector is for "smart people" and "well-balanced" people, not me. But, there is plenty of room in the tech sector for anyone willing to look around for his or her niche.

CHAPTER 5

Body Postures and Gestures on the Job

An "impairment" in body posture may be both in the form of an inability to read another's posture and in an inability to express what you wish to express through body language. One quick example I observed recently of improper body posture leading to problems follows:

Steve was leaning over a desk helping an employee fix her computer. Since he was focused only on the computer and not the woman in the chair, he stood comfortably and placed his left hand on the back of the chair and his right hand on the mouse while fixing the computer.

This opened up his chest area towards the woman, communicating a sexual openness that he did not intend to communicate. I stepped in quickly and explained clearly, "Steve, when your chest area is open to a person like that (modeling body position), it indicates intimacy. Instead, when you lean over a desk, it is best to place both hands on or near the desk area, which allows a wall in-between you and the person you are helping. It keeps that professional distance we all need. Thanks."

The situation was addressed and the miscommunication was cleared. Steve was grateful for the quick, clear, blunt feedback and perhaps he will remember this feedback next time he is positioning himself in a similar situation.

That said, it is not likely he will remember without significant effort. When there is a problem, Steve has laser focus in fixing the problem. When that problem is in a piece of computer software, watch out. Steve's complete attention disappears into fixing the problem.

Best Practice 8: "Quiet" Posture

Recently, a former FBI Special Agent, Navarro, wrote a book titled *What Every BODY is Saying: An Ex-FBI Agent's Guide to Speed-Reading People* (Navarro and Karlins 2008). In a brilliant way, Navarro compares non-verbal language to a computer program, saying that we can essentially download this information about body posture so any of us can have superior ability to read and interpret the hidden subtext of nonverbal messages present in any conversation.

But while you are working on your ability to read body language, you need an immediate solution that will make your day-to-day work easier.

The "Quiet" Posture Best Practice comes from Michael, my husband. He has managed to avoid body language miscommunication 90 percent of the time. Where most people with difficulties in this area would get into trouble, Michael is relatively safe from difficulty.

First, a definition of "quiet" body posture. Quiet posture is putting your body in a position that communicates nothing; it is a "mute" body posture.

Normally, a person's body posture communicates many things. If you stand close to someone, you like them (or are trying to intimidate them). If you distance yourself from them you probably do not like them. If you distance yourself and hold your nose high, you are indicating that you think the other person is far less important than you or smells bad.

So, if a person cannot read body language or portray proper body language himself, what is a person to do? You can always learn, clinically and slowly, what people usually mean when they move a certain way.

It has been my experience that learning body language on a clinical study is not as effective as it needs to be for the work environment. The error rate for properly expressing oneself is too high for me to recommend learning body language as the first and only step.

Instead, I recommend developing a "quiet" body posture. This is a body posture that, according to the books and social rules on what certain postures communicate, communicates as little as possible. Your body positioning is neutral. Someone looking at you would not know if you are happy, sad, excited, scared, or any other emotion because your body posture communicates essentially nothing.

Quiet body posture will look different depending on your size, general personality, and typical way of interacting. Here is an example of Michael's quiet body posture:

1. Arms relaxed at side, hands half-way in pockets.

2. Shoulders relaxed.

3. Feet not too close, not too far apart from each other, hip-distance from each other, with one slightly in front of the other.

4. One knee bent which tips one hip to the side slightly.

5. Chin not up, not down, just neutral in the middle.

6. Head resting comfortably on spine, pulled back slightly.

Depending on the shape of your body, a quiet posture may be one with your hands at your sides. Or perhaps your arms folded across the front of your body (although this usually communicates that you are closed off). The way to find the quietest posture for yourself is to ask a few trusted friends "What do you think this communicates?" while making the particular posture. As you try different body positions, you will eventually receive the answer of "That position doesn't communicate anything" and you will be able to put together your new quiet posture.

Why is a quiet posture so important? It is easy for others to misjudge a body posture that is out of sync with the situation. It is much harder to misjudge nothing.

The basic steps are:

Stay for 30 seconds to a minute. To come up, inhale, press the back heel firmly into the floor, and reach up through the arms, straightening the right knee. Turn the feet forward and release the arms with an exhalation, or keep them extended upward for more challenge. Take a few breaths, then turn the feet to the left and repeat for the same length. When you are finished return to *Tadasana*—stand straight, feet close together, arms hanging loosely at your sides, eyes looking forward at nothing in particular.

As the instructor gives each body part's position, you are able to adjust as needed. You have the visual input of other class members who are also adjusting their bodies to match the pose. You probably have a full length mirror in which you can see where your body is in space and adjust as needed.

The mirror gives you tremendous feedback. With a bit of practice, yoga or other similar slow movement classes can be a perfect training ground for people with AS who wish to develop better body awareness. Unless you work exclusively at your home office, body awareness is critical in your work environment.

In my own area, Berkeley, California, I do yoga three to four times per week and often there are in attendance many adults with varying shades of autism, many of whom are thriving in their respective careers. As they walk in, I see the tippy toe walk, and as they walk out, their feet are usually flat, walking with a more relaxed "standard" gait. I see people who will probably never give me eye contact even if we do yoga together for years. I see them coming in with a little tell-tale hand flap and I see them leaving calm, recentered and ready to face another overwhelming day.

To supplement your work, study people with quiet posture. On a weekend or some day when you have free time, go to a local park or other area where you can see people. If you are in a low density population area, watch TV for examples. As you watch people, look at whether their body language is loud or quiet.

Rule: If a person makes large movements, fast movements, or many movements, their body language is probably loud. Ignore them.

Unless you are narcissistic, you probably do not want to draw attention to yourself on purpose.

Note that people with autism are sometimes misdiagnosed narcissistic due to mindblindness issues. The key differentiating factor is that a person with AS mindblindness is simply physically blind. A person with narcissism has "mindblindness with a purpose." Someone with a diagnosis of narcissism experiences such intense feelings of superiority and delusions of grandeur that other people are too unimportant to recognize. A narcissist person takes advantage of others in order to meet his own selfish needs. For a person with AS, this type of manipulation is not only unfeasible, but a waste of time.

If a person makes few, small, slow movements, their body language is probably quiet. Most people will not be consistently one or the other although people tend towards loudness or quietness.

Watch the quiet people. Study their movements. Mimic their movements. Feel how your body moves, or does not move, as you adjust your posture to mimic theirs. This is kinesthetic role playing and it will serve you well long-term.

If you feel hesitant to do this exercise, thinking that it is too immature or silly, consider that most highly professional adults have done these exact things in order to achieve success in their careers. How you move your body is important.

For example, as a young woman, I briefly attended modeling school. I learned how to walk confidently there. We did the exact same exercises that I am asking you to do now—practice body movements that fit what impression you want to give. Adjust your shoulders, your arms, your legs. Practice movement (or a calm lack of movement).

Nearly anyone with a public-facing career has, at some point, practiced these basic body positioning skills. Please, dear reader, do not consider this to be an immature exercise. Allow yourself the benefit of being a professional, even if you are not treated as one yet.

The final step is to practice quiet body posture until you can do it easily. You can safely master this ability in the quiet of your own home, in a controlled environment where you can adjust your posture with the aid of a mirror, preferably full body length. Even your reflection in a large window or sliding glass door will suffice.

After you have mastered it in a safe environment, try slowly calming down your posture at work. Do not do it suddenly, especially if you were a loud body posture person before. Slowly adjust.

My husband uses this technique. His body posture is extremely quiet. He is rarely misunderstood.

Rule: It is not always possible to correct misunderstandings. It is best to avoid them in the first place. Using a mute body posture avoids the problems by not providing a way for them to become visible.

Best Practice 9: Mimic Other
Successful Professionals

Once you have developed the ability to achieve and maintain quiet body posture, you will always have this ability as your fall-back, default position when times get rough. As discussed earlier in the book, Maslow's pyramid illustrates how important it is to have basic needs met first. The first step is to develop quiet posture as part of your basic needs fulfillment.

You can now move on to step two, developing good career-oriented body posture. In every field, there is an "ideal" body movement, a way to carry your body that communicates the personality needed to get that particular job done. Let's contrast two careers so we can it is hoped, see the difference in body posture: politicians and research scientists.

First, politicians spend most of their time with their eyes up, looking at people. Scientists often spend their time with their eyes down, looking at an experiment, a laptop screen, or an article, book, or magazine. Assuming that the bulk of the scientist's work is based in a lab, the scientist is probably giving only a few presentations every few years: when he needs new grants and when he presents his research findings. The vast majority of his time is spent in non-self-presentation work.

The difference between the daily work in each career affects the position of their shoulders, head, and neck. Over time, it even changes the body's actual shape. If a scientist is hunched over a table for many hours, his spine adjusts. If a politician is conscientiously keeping his body erect and spine straight in order to communicate strength and openness to his constituents, his spine adjusts and muscles are strengthened to keep this body posture in that particularly upright form.

A politician generally has a body posture that is wide-open, welcoming, and alert. His shoulders are wide; his hands are out actively communicating through gestures; and his head is solidly up, facing the public.

In comparison, a research scientist will often adjust his body to the most comfortable position that is appropriate for his particular body shape. The scientist's various body parts—shoulders, arms, legs, neck—will adjust to whatever type of research is needed in that scientist's particular lab. Over time, with a career that involves looking down at a table throughout the day, it is likely a slight hunch will form at the top of the spine. There will also be a squint in the eyes from a tendency to look at the paperwork or computer rather than the people. There may also be a lack of gestures since the research findings tell the story, not the scientist's hands.

When your posture does not match your job position it can sometimes lead to difficulties. For example, Mark is a programmer who deeply enjoys coding for eight to nine hours a day, but since he works out at the gym regularly, he has good, open, straight body posture. The workouts are necessary for him to keep his sensory system under control. If he skips a week or even a few days, he becomes agitated and easily sent into sensory overload. With regular workouts, Mark's sensory system appears to be more resilient.

Over the years Mark's bosses have continually tried to promote him to management positions. When Mark has refused the management positions (without the awareness of the miscommunication between his body posture and his boss's interpretation of that posture) Mark has been seen as a lazy employee. Mark's posture communicated that he was a go-getter.

If Mark had recognized the disconnect, he could have made a slight adjustment, perhaps putting his hands deep in his pockets more often, crossing his arms more often, or even shifting his shoulders slightly forward to protect the chest area—the area that often communicates openness.

Instead, Mark was confused and it affected his job. He did not get the pay raises he wanted because, by his boss's judgement, Mark was lazy. The great work that he was doing in his current position was significantly diminished in perceived value because of this simple miscommunication.

In 1981 Allan Pease wrote a book titled *Body Language: How to Read Others' Thoughts by Their Gestures.* This was the first large attempt at making the public aware of the non-verbal meaning behind their gestures. Since then, the field has been well-researched and there are plenty of great resources to teach you how to read gestures and how to make appropriate gestures. It may not come naturally, but it can be learned.

While some areas of social interaction are so complex that coping strategies and work-arounds are most appropriate, when it comes to gestures, it may be worth your time to study them so you can use them fully.

A few reasons why gestures are worthy of study:

1. Hand gestures are less complex than full body gestures.

2. Given that hand gestures are limited to only two appendages, mastering the message is more easily within grasp.

3. Hand gestures are a very powerful method of communication.

4. If you can have "normal" hand gestures, it is more likely that others will judge your actions and intentions as you hope they will be judged.

I wish I could give a full list of hand gestures in this book but I do not have the space for such a task. I will give a condensed list that will I hope be of considerable help:

- *Both palms up*—Part of a pleading, requesting, asking posture. Used for requesting a hug when arms are also outstretched.

- *Hands holding each other*—You are centered, decided, comfortable with yourself and your decisions.

- *Arms crossed*—Protective, feeling overwhelmed. If you are talking to someone with their arms crossed, consider ending the conversation. There is a good chance the person is only listening politely but would rather stop talking or listening.

- *Hands moving in front of you while talking*—You are passionate about the message you are trying to communicate.

- *Hands on hips*—Trying to establish dominance or force a point. This is not a good posture to use unless you need it for some specific purpose. People who habitually put their hands on their hips are often seen as bossy or controlling.

- *One hand on chin*—Thinking, pensive. This is a nice posture if you are in a conversation with someone and want to communicate that you are really listening and considering what they are saying.

Sometimes, despite your best intentions, your hand gestures will communicate something you never intended to communicate. Here is one personal example from one wonderfully brilliant man with AS who honestly, truly intended to communicate something other than what his hand gestures indicated.

A full 21 years ago, when my husband asked me to marry him, he had his hands in his pockets. We were sitting on a couch and his hands were fully in his pockets. In proposals you see on TV, the

During the next presentation Sarah used a bandage to tape her middle and third finger together. She was not sure she could follow through on this new habit while under the stress of giving a presentation. The bandage looked normal enough. No one asked about it; they just assumed she had a cut on her fingers.

Sarah did her regular presentation but this time she pointed at various parts of the slides as she talked about them. Sure enough, the audience was engaged and did not ask as many unimportant questions. Sarah was a bit surprised at how good she felt when she walked out. People treated her nicely after the presentation. Sarah remembers thinking, "So this is what it feels like to have people like you."

Sarah enjoyed it enough that it was easy for her to point appropriately from then on. Over the next few months she began using the pointing gesture in everyday conversation.

Sarah did notice from time to time that she used the middle finger by mistake. It always happened when she was agitated or annoyed with the person she was talking to. She was aware that it was a Freudian slip on her part, showing a "bad sign" to someone who was being unpleasant with her.

Sarah's example is one of self-awareness followed by self-training until an old, ineffective interaction pattern became a useful, successful pattern of behavior.

You may have a hand or arm gesture that is ineffective and cannot be replaced. This is OK. Just as with body language, using "quiet" hand gestures can sometimes be the best choice in a work environment.

When given the choice between a large wrong gesture and a small wrong gesture, choose the smaller one. For example, Tom is accustomed to making a large motion that involves rolling his shoulders, straightening his spine, and cracking his neck to the side. Tom's friends are accustomed to the gesture, but at work, with so many people around, Tom makes the motion as small and unnoticeable as possible. He wears button-down shirts instead of t-shirts to partially hide the shoulder roll and he tries to keep his spine straight most of the day so there is not a significant flux when he gestures.

How you gesture is part of your personal character. In a work setting, a calm, professional persona is probably most appropriate for most jobs. Small and calm gestures are the most professional and also the safest.

As one Aspie teenager working at a research science lab explained, "Gestures are like the steering wheel. Turn it fast and you'll crash. If you turn the wheel right, well not 'right' because then you would have to turn it left to get back on track, if you turn it *well*, you can steer the conversation where you want it to go. It's awesome." This teen has become particularly good at body language since he has studied it "as hard as I studied for Calculus last year."

The wonderful thing about body language is that it is pretty much universal. Your location, culture, and spoken language do not change the gestures needed much. The level of acceptable emotion behind the gestures may change, but arms crossed in America means the same thing as arms crossed in Italy. Gestures can be a wonderfully easy way to make social situations at work more successful.

CHAPTER 6

The People You Work With

What are "peer relationships" in a work environment? For starters, the standard definitions for peer relationships are usually referring to children. There is a vast difference between appropriate peer relationships on the playground and appropriate peer relationships at work.

You have a distinct benefit if you did not fully master appropriate peer relationships on the playground. Playground friendships will not be a default strategy for you. They will not come naturally and you will be better positioned to do what you need to do at work.

If you work in an office setting, you will probably observe many people who use playground rules in a professional environment and it does not work well for them.

The value of friendly little conversations becomes less important when you weigh it against your ability to communicate your need for a raise, your need for a different position in the company, or many other communications that affect your happiness on the job. These conversations, if they took their playground form, would be entirely ineffective.

Best Practice 11: The Back-Stabber, the Drama Queen, and the Glory Hog

In most work environments, there is a mix of people who are difficult to deal with no matter how socially savvy you are. In Stan's work, he often felt like he was surrounded by freaks. He found this amusing since he had grown up with kids telling him he was the freak. Yet, now as an adult in a stable career as a researcher, Stan felt more "normal" than ever. It was the antics of the people around him that seemed odd.

One year, a new researcher, Zach, was hired who often claimed that he had done the hard work behind projects that were actually completed by other people. During meetings, Zach would present the results as if he was the only one working on them. While everyone experienced emotional strain due to Zach's Glory Hog antics, Stan felt only amusement. On Stan's internal meter of "what's important," these relationships with peers and colleagues ranked very low. As a result, Stan was able to stay focused on his work while others worried, causing themselves to experience a decrease in productivity.

In one meeting, Zach took credit for a project that Stan had been working on for two years. During a short pause in Zach's presentation, Stan said in a calm, slightly amused voice, "He's insane. This was my project. He had nothing to do with it." Stan said this in such a logical, clear, and emotionless voice that it sounded like the truth even though it was such a strong claim. When asked, Stan was able to give the details, explaining that Zach had been claiming credit for others' projects ever since he had been hired. Stan listed the other projects that had been inappropriately credited to Zach. Upon hearing this, Zach, like a typical Glory Hog, became defensive and furious, experiencing a strong emotional reaction. Management saw that the Glory Hog was out of control and dismissed him from the meeting.

After getting input from the rest of the team, management took corrective action. The Glory Hog was summarily fired and the rest of the team was so grateful for Stan's ability to speak the truth when the rest of them were so upset. The others had not spoken up because, when Zach was first hired, one of the team members had tried to alert management to what Zach was doing, but she was moved immediately to a different team. Management had not

Your relationship with your boss is—most likely—the most important relationship you have at your workplace. The most important aspect of that relationship is: *respect*.

Before your boss can respect you, you have to habitually respect yourself.

Here is one story of a man who was not able to achieve his potential until he started respecting himself: Aaron had always been anti-social. He considered it part of his personality and did not have any plans to change it until he got his first job. He managed to get his dream job programming for a game company.

Aaron wanted to fit in so he went to lunch with the guys even when the socialization was unpleasant. He went to the company parties even though it was such a sensory nightmare that he had to use the restroom to throw up when the lights and sounds became too much. Aaron tried to participate in conversations but he was always on the outside trying to keep up with the conversation.

For nearly a year, Aaron pushed himself past his limits. Aaron did not have any direction in how to do these new social tasks—he just did what he thought might be right. He felt like he was experiencing an intense culture shock and he often felt nauseous and sick. He often "zoned out," only waking when a co-worker was waving a hand in front of Aaron's face while saying, "Hello? Anybody in there?" Aaron's co-workers were nice people, but they did not understand what was "wrong" with Aaron.

When Aaron went home to visit family over the holidays, Aaron's mom and dad expressed concern. The first thing Aaron's mom said when greeting him at the door was, "Oh! You look awful!" Aaron was not offended, just curious why she would say that. Aaron had not noticed a change.

Once his family pointed it out, Aaron noticed that he had gained a considerable amount of weight and his skin looked pale. He had new wrinkles on his face and his general appearance was bedraggled. Aaron talked to his parents about his job. While talking to them Aaron realized he needed to change something at work. The last thing Aaron's dad said as Aaron was walking out the door was "Son, take care of yourself."

When Aaron returned to work, he started "taking care" of himself. He did what was most comfortable to him. Aaron focused on his work, walking straight to his desk in the mornings, not stopping to chat with colleagues. Aaron said "Thanks, but I'm busy" to all invitations. Aaron's colleagues did not object. They had sensed Aaron's discomfort and were relieved not to have Aaron in their group.

Within a few months Aaron felt like his old self again. He was now a more valuable part of the team and was performing up to the level his boss had hoped Aaron would when he had first hired Aaron.

Respect yourself and you will be more likely to find a boss who respects you in return. This respect will lead to many beneficial things, mostly the freedom to work in the way you naturally work best.

There are few generalizations that can be made about how to deal effectively with the person who is managing you. Rules that work in one job are the wrong ones to use in a different job. The only generalization that works across the scope of all employment and all cultures is the above advice—respect yourself, treat your boss with respect, and one hopes you will be similarly treated with the respect you need to thrive at work.

Best Practice 13: "Get a Life!"

When you choose a career, you are also choosing a particular lifestyle. It helps to take a step back and look analytically at who you are and what you want from your life, then match the career to what you want most.

A clear case-in-point follows.

Shawn in San Francisco was recently made partner at a prestigious law firm. She managed to achieve this career success by ignoring her lack of "peer relationships." She did not marry. She did not have children. Her only friends were those who furthered her career.

While some may see her life as "not a life at all," it fits her perfectly. Shawn says, "Every day I say to myself, 'This is what I always wanted and I love it.'" Shawn would not have been able to achieve what she wanted if she had not maintained the focus needed for the seemingly endless work days. She may not have been able to sustain complete devotion to her career if she had been burdened by the thought that she needed to have friends in order to be normal.

Shawn's professional success is unquestionable. She charges $480/hr and has nearly complete control over what she does with her time. She has an assistant who now does the work she dislikes doing (going outside the building to get lunch, running errands, answering the phone). While personally I have different life goals than Shawn does, I can see how her autistic ability to focus helped her bulldoze her way through the obstacles that many women face in such time-intensive fields.

When people say to Shawn "Sure you made partner, but you have no life," Shawn just laughs and stays silent. She knows that most people cannot understand how little appeal is behind that "life" to which they are referring.

There are many fringe benefits of Shawn's "failure" to form appropriate peer relationships. Because Shawn was "so busy trying to make partner" she was able to avoid many, many social engagements over the years. She was able to skip family reunions that were "pure hell" for her. Shawn's family easily accepted this and bragged to relatives that "Shawn works at ___ law firm in downtown San Francisco."

Also, Shawn was able to bypass the terrifying prospect of having a child. While she probably would have had a beautiful baby if she had tried, she knew that an infant would push her dangerously past complete sensory overload. More than once, hearing a child crying in the grocery store had sent Shawn running out of the store without her groceries. (Now as we have seen Shawn has an assistant to do this for her.)

Shawn was also able to avoid the confusion and difficulties of having to live with someone, marry someone. Her comment was,

"I can barely stand living with myself. How would I put up with a second person?" She works with enough people during the day that, by the time she gets home, the relaxation and quietness is "delicious."

If you happen to be forming a career that makes people comment that it will come at the expense of "having a real life," take a minute to consider the specifics to which they are referring.

CHAPTER 7

Do I Enjoy My Job?

There is an infectious quality to enjoying your job. Imagine the two following scenarios as an interesting way to judge your own response to this social effect:

Scenario 1: You are in a meeting with 14 other people. The person leading the meeting, Dave, stands up and says, "I am so glad you are all here. I would like to show you something about our upcoming deadline.

"It's 3pm, right? So you are all probably a little tired, maybe a little hungry, maybe ready for the day to be over, right? Well, I am going to use a few visual aids to show you how important our upcoming deadline is. I hope it will help you see how much we all want this project to rock. If we are able to finish only the basic features by next Thursday, it will be like giving our client a pretzel as a snack."

Dave passed out one tiny pretzel stick to each person at the meeting. Most people ate theirs.

"If we can finish the list of extra features, it will be like giving our client a much nicer gift, a cookie. My friend made these..."

Dave passed out some yummy-looking oatmeal and raisin cookies. They looked good, but were small. Most people ate theirs in a single bite.

"Now, if we can finish this list of above-and-beyond features... (Dave turns on a visual presentation at the front of the room showing a short list of extra features that will require extra work, but still be quite doable before the deadline.) If we can finish these features, we can show our client that we are worth our weight in gold. Or at least a bit of weight in chocolate."

Dave gave to each person a 5lb bar of the most delicious chocolate that was available in their city. The bar was heavy, nicely wrapped, and a very clear symbol of what Dave wanted to convey— that good sensations are associated with doing an extra great job.

You are in this meeting and you happen to love chocolate. As you open the bar, the smell overcomes your senses and you let out a little moan by mistake. You are not the only one who does so. As Dave continues the slideshow, you nibble off your massive 5lb bar of chocolate.

Scenario 2: It is 3pm on a different day, different project, different boss. The boss starts his presentation by reading off the first slide. Then the second, then the third. There is nothing visual for you to see except the words on the slides, which actually do not make much sense without more information, but the presenter does not give more information—he just reads the slide.

You start to doze off and 30 minutes later you wake with a start when the lights are turned back on. You have no idea what the presentation was about.

During which meeting would you have felt the most enjoyment? During which would you have learned something more about your job and what you needed to do?

Note that, with AS, perceptions of enjoyment can be less predictable. For example, when describing the two scenarios to other people with AS, one woman said, "I'd want to be in the presentation where I got a nap! Of course, the nap! What I would give for a chance to snooze for 30 minutes at 3pm on a work day!"

So, this question is not perfect; its purpose is simply to help you think about whether or not one person's enthusiasm and excitement about something affects you in some way.

b. Uneasiness or a negative emotion

c. Panic

7. When you are getting ready for work, are you:

a. focused on getting ready (even if getting ready does not come easy for you)?

b. feeling enough dread that getting ready is quite difficult?

c. so unfocused that you are not fully aware of what you are doing?

If you got five or more A answers, you are probably in a career that is healthy and good for you. If you answered two or fewer As, perhaps it is time to review the career books listed in the Further Reading section along with other resources mentioned in this book.

Note that the questionnaire does not ask:

- Do you have to work hard to "pretend to be normal"? (A term coined by Liane Holliday Willey.)

  → It is a given that you will probably have to work hard to interact in a world with people who do not have similarly autistic brains. You may be lucky enough to have a career with a high prevalence of people with Asperger Syndrome, but you most likely will be in an environment where you need to make many adjustments to communicate effectively and work with others.

- Do you have a meltdown at the end of the day?

  → This is not a sign of a bad career. In fact, it is a common experience that crosses over all types of people (although the meltdown for others is probably far less severe). Many people in high-pressure careers "crash" at the end of the day. This is why night-time TV and other relaxation-oriented activities are so popular. As long as the healing strategies are not self-destructive and the release of stress is not hurting the other people you live with, the meltdown may be a natural part of dealing with life.

- How often are you pushed "past your limit"?
    → It is likely that you are always past your limit. This is a deeply regrettable state of being, but I cannot in good conscience state that a person with Asperger Syndrome can and should find a career so ideal that you can stay balanced throughout the day. The world is not that kind.

Best Practice 16: Avoiding the
Biggest—Abdicating Free Will

Perhaps the biggest potential for error in career choice for a person with Asperger Syndrome is the easy assumption that someone else is in charge of your career. Here is how this mistake happens:

1. *Overload.* The person with AS, no matter the age or stage of career, is on complete overload with sensory input, mental chaos, and the ensuing internal panic.

2. *Self-preservation.* In complete mental chaos, he naturally and subconsciously switches his efforts to self-preservation.

3. *Abdication.* When all his energies are being focused on surviving overload, he has no mental space left to consider options that would normally be his to make. He abdicates them to whomever is nearby and can make the decision for him.

Let's take a look at this in real life, a personal example and unfortunately one that occurred nearly every day for many years. To preface this example, note that, as adults, my husband and I had two jobs at any given time: the money-earning job and the job of parent. The job of wage-earner was mostly to support the job of raising our children. As I refer to home life, please know that I am referring to it the same way I would refer to a paying job.

There were seasons where I scheduled it so the children and I were not home when Michael arrived home. If home life was simply too chaotic, if the kids were in a phase of development that was particularly difficult, we had to eliminate that original impact.

There were holidays, many holidays actually, when he worked through most of the holiday, then as soon as his vacation started, I would leave on vacation with two of the children, leaving two with him. There were summers when I literally disappeared for a while with the children. I spent one summer in New Zealand traveling up and down the coast while my husband survived his last summer working for a big company. It was that summer that convinced him that working in a smaller office was a necessary solution no matter the pay cut. He might not have been able to fully realize this if he had been devoting his limited post-workday energies to interacting with his children.

The summer after our third child was born, I traveled with my newborn and two older sons during most of the summer—just roaming with no particular end point in mind.

The summer after our fourth and final child was born, my husband announced a deadline that would be an inferno to us as a couple. So, I threw the tent in the car, five sleeping bags, and drove away in our little minivan for 32 days of camping across the western US. We drove through 14 different states and changed diapers at nearly every rest stop. As a group of siblings, the children bonded on a level that was deeper than I ever dared hope possible.

It was yet another flip side to the coin. If my husband was a neurotypical then perhaps I would not have been pushed to such a seemingly desperate solution. If he was like our neighbors, he would have worked a bit of overtime, but come home and played with our children in the evenings. We would have lived a typical life, with the children separate in their own rooms at night, not interacting with each other. The children's tendency not to bond with each other would have been solidified.

Instead, I got to run a sort of Boot Camp for Siblings on the Spectrum. In the confines of the minivan, my little Stephen, who was struggling to learn language due to his hyperlexia, had one big brother sitting on each side. As we drove through the forests of the Pacific Northwest, they said—in stereo—"Tree. Tree. Tree. Tree. Tree. Tree. Tree. Tree. Tree..." what seemed like thousands of times. They taught him "Car," a great word for freeway travel, "Sky," and "Ocean." In performing this much-needed act of service for their little brother (speech and language therapy bombardment style), they developed an ultra strong sibling bond.

> *Wise men know this truth: the only way to help yourself is to help others.*
>
> *—Elbert Hubbard in The Philistine*

The two older brothers learned crucial social skills and familial skills that will help them immensely when they have children of their own. For little Stephen, it was an every-waking-hour session of social skills, SLP, OT, BT, ABA that lasted all summer.

For my little newborn Suzetta, she was only three months, so she slept through most of the trip, but it is not surprising that now, at eight years old, she is an experienced traveler on several continents.

The purpose of this small tangent in this work-related book is to show the immense immediate benefits of AS can trickle down to the other people in your life. The AS limitations provided the initial push for a tremendously beneficial experience.

During that summer, I gained a sense of confidence that I had never had before. I realized that, if I could go camping with an infant, a toddler, and two older brothers, I could handle just about anything that came my way. Michael had the freedom to exist in an empty home for 32 days, long enough for him, at approximately 25 days, to realize that he liked his family better at home than not at home.

Over the years we found that both the extreme solution worked and the temporary, in-the-moment solutions worked. There were years at a time when Michael "had to work late" nearly every night of the week. He also worked through weekends. It was not ideal, not at all, but it was a survival strategy that allowed a perfectly wonderful man with Asperger Syndrome to experience the deep, primal satisfaction of having children. As they grew and as Michael's sensory system became more balanced, Michael was able to handle more input and the children became a larger and larger part of his life.

In case this gives you hope: Michael is now able to get two of the children off to school in the morning, making them a healthy breakfast, talking with them, and giving them the sense that their father loves them and cares about their academic success. He often picks up the other two children from school at the end of the day.

Michael works late only once or twice a month. He is home on weekends. The overload is always a possibility, but it occurs only rarely, approximately once a week, and is often easily averted or otherwise softened.

Now, to carryover this concept to the workplace environment. Abdicating free will may be happening to you more often than you care to admit. Think back to the last company meeting you attended. Were you able to voice your opinion freely? Were you able to get the resources you needed to complete your work well?

Overload causes a tendency to give up your free will or at the very least it limits your available choices. Below are a few coping strategies that will help you retain your choices while allowing for the inevitable overload.

When presented with a choice, rather than ignoring it or letting someone else decide, say:

1. "Can I get back to you on that later today?"

2. "That's an important question. I need to look into a few things before I answer."

3. "I am in the middle of a different project right now and need to stay focused. Can I answer you later?"

Keep several appropriate pre-scripted answers at the ready so that, next time you feel yourself melting into survival mode, you are ready to protect your choices so you can resurface without having sacrificed anything too terribly important.

Best Practice 17: Career Trajectory

A Best Practice that will help keep your career aligned with your desires is to actually draft out your career. Use your visualization skills to craft a career trajectory. Many people plan out their careers by setting goals and doing what it takes to reach those goals. For example, when I was young I knew that I wanted to be a writer, an athlete, an elementary teacher, an entrepreneur, a manager, a mother, a professor, and a designer. So far, I have managed six out of eight. (Note that my trajectory was not linear. Many people with AS who have a love of routine may prefer a more linear career path.)

If you "think in pictures" as many people with autism do, it may help bring form to your career if you map it out. If you are intensely focused on one career and one career only, perhaps this map may look direct and unswerving.

For one man with AS, he sketched his life out as follows:

- Age 25: Bachelor's degree from UC Berkeley

- Age 32: PhD from Stanford

- Age 42: Professor at MIT

- Age 62: Retire.

This time-line was enough for him. He met his goals with a few changes. (One university rejected him so he went with his second choice.)

Many people I know use a far more detailed path, listing a lifetime plan, 10 year plan, 5 year plan, and 1 year plan. The shorter the length of the plan is, the greater the level of detail.

Every New Year's Eve take a pencil in your hand and write down your new, revised career trajectory. Review the previous year's trajectory and see how close you have come.

This exercise helps you not only identify your career goals, but it helps you see that often you get what you want in this crazy, overwhelming world.

A note of caution: If you experience frustration when a goal is unmet or needs to change, you can do several things to ease the frustration.

1. You can replace the unmet goal with a new one.

2. You can have a back-up strategy for when the pressure becomes difficult to bear—do a particularly calming activity such as running, sleeping, or whatever your body finds calming.

3. Do not do this particular activity in the first place. If the frustration of an unmet goal is too frustrating, then the purpose of this exercise is lost.

This exercise is meant to give you a mental framework to guide you as you make everyday choices. It is not meant to increase the difficulty of your life.

CHAPTER 8

Your Most Valuable Traits

You have many valuable traits. Recognizing them and enhancing them is one of your main tasks as an adult. Let's compare two brothers who both have mild shades of AS. Theo sees himself as a "slow learner" and he rarely tries anything new. Rex was also dubbed a "slow learner" in school, but he ignored what the teachers wrote on his report card and instead focused on his valuable traits. You can probably guess that Theo was in a low-paying dead-end job (a job that has no hope of advancement or increase in pay) while Rex's career had sky-rocketed.

At a holiday family dinner, Rex and Theo had the following conversation (paraphrased):

Rex: "So, Theo, how is your job these days?"

Theo: "Fine."

Rex: "Do you think you'll stay at the same job for...a long time?"

Theo: "Yeah, of course. It fits me. It's OK."

Rex: "But bro, you have skills you could really use at a better job. Like, remember when you and I built that remote control cat-shaped robot when we were kids? You used all sorts of materials to make the outer shell. And when I couldn't figure out how to make the legs work, you're the one who figured it out. We never got it walking right, but it did move. That was you bro. The robotics industry is booming right now. They could really use someone like you. Now you're just flipping burgers." (Note: "Flipping burgers" is a colloquial term used to define a job where you do a non-intellectual, manual labor that is completely routinized.)

Theo: "I'm not flipping burgers!"

Rex: "Well, you're doing the same thing you were doing ten years ago. What happened?"

Theo: "Hey, back off. I'm doing what I can."

Did you catch those last five words? When I heard them, they resonated in my ears very loudly. I can still hear them. "*I'm doing what I can.*" The difference between these two brothers is that one chose to focus on his best talents and one chose to define his ability (what he *can* do) by his limitations.

Best Practice 18: Know Your Strengths

In accounting, management, and other areas of business there is a common knowledge rule, "You cannot grow what you cannot measure."

If you do not know your strengths, how can you present them as valuable qualities when interviewing for jobs or asking for a raise? Recognizing your strengths may not come naturally to someone who does not spend much time on introspection. That is OK. Just find a way to explore your strengths in other ways.

Recognizing the AS-ness in your way of existing in the world will help you immensely. Reading books such as this one and others will help give you further context. Understanding how your brain works is the most valuable thing you can do to boost your career. Seek understanding for how you work and why you work that way. Within this context, you can identify your strengths.

If you don't recognize your strengths, you can't emphasize them on the job. A few anecdotal examples of how this applies in business. If you do not track your budget, you cannot grow your company (except by luck alone). If you do not measure your progress, you have very little sense of what progress has been made.

This rule is an important one to grasp, especially when dealing with AS. You have many, many strengths. These strengths are often portrayed as weaknesses in common settings. You must focus hard on the benefits of your way of being if you are going to grow those benefits into a productive, happy, solid career.

Using pen and paper (or a computer or any other recording instrument), write down as many of your strengths as you can think of. Forget the negative comments you have heard in the past.

Make this list as quickly as you can without becoming stressed. Write anything that possibly could be considered a strength. For example, one woman with AS doing this activity wrote:

- Generally happy.

- Smart.

- Far too talkative!

- Can't seem to stop talking.

- Enjoy being around people but don't notice if they enjoy being around me.

- Opinionated.

Her list started out with positive strengths, but quickly degenerated into the typical put-downs she had heard all her life.

But, she kept going, kept writing, and it is a good thing she did. After she had brainstormed for more than 20 ideas, she was able to rework the list to focus on strengths.

- Strong ability to form long sentences.

- Enjoys a high level of speech during the day.

- Go-getter.

- Strong analytical ability and desire to stand up for quality.

- And so forth.

In reworking the list, she took the negatives and looked at their flip side. As she opened up to recognizing her strengths, she realized a whole new career path for herself, a far more satisfying career path than the one she had at that time. She had been filing medical records in a doctor's office for years and would often get in trouble for chatting with co-workers, or more specifically, "talking to" workers, not "talking *with*" them. More than once she had heard co-workers complaining behind her back that she had been "droning on and on." Her job would have been far more suited to someone shy who enjoyed not speaking.

After reviewing her list, she made a delightful realization. She was far better suited for a job in sales. She started in telemarketing where she was able to speak almost non-stop for eight hours a day. She became one of the more successful employees because she was the only one in the office who did not mind repeating the same script over and over again.

After a few years, she moved on to bigger and better sales jobs, all of them over the phone so she did not have issues with face-to-face interaction. She is a passionate sales person, well paid since she is on commission, and finally she is able to come home at the end of a work day happy and satisfied.

She is mildly dissatisfied that she does not have any enduring friendships beyond those brief contacts she makes when she lands a sale, but in general, she is finding ways to make her life as satisfying as possible. Her next goal is to learn how to keep friends long-term.

Best Practice 19: How You
Help Your Team Focus

There is a reason why TV shows often portray the less successful people in an office sitting around chatting, hanging around the water cooler. In the late 80s, when people in the US started drinking bottled water, many offices purchased water coolers. The water coolers became a magnet for people who wanted a break from their work.

Here is how the dialogue goes inside a non-autistic brain:

1. "I've been working on this project a full half hour."

2. "I can't concentrate anymore."

3. "What can I do that will still look like work but give me a break from actually doing anything? The water cooler!"

The social interaction that occurs around the water cooler is very similar to "playground speak."

At the playground, the child has no specific objective, no deadline, no paid project to complete, so he can interact casually with other kids.

At the water cooler, the employee is trying to avoid the specific objective, avoid the deadline, and avoid the paid project that he needs to complete. The conversation at the water cooler is rarely anything except big people engaging in playground spcak.

One problem—as a boss, I do not want to see any of my employees goofing off. I am in charge of making sure the company can survive the next quarter and it is hoped, thrive. Every minute that an employee spends at the water cooler is another minute lost. Yes, the brain needs breaks from work in order to function effectively, but I have not come across a study yet that shows that standing by a water cooler is an effective way to recharge. In my office, I do not have a water cooler and I never will.

Summary: If there are not any obvious, pressing benefits to a particular type of social interaction, consider that:

- It might actually be beneficial to abstain.

- It may be easier for you to abstain, leaving more energy for other, more pleasing things.

- Abstaining from some peer relationships can increase your value at work.

It is a good idea to determine whether extending yourself socially to an uncomfortable degree is detracting from your ability to perform your job.

in suburbia, I could have easily spent 30 hours a week doing things with friends: dinners, volunteer work, taking the kids to the park, working in the back yard with a friend chatting while gardening. Now that I am living in the city, we spend only a few minutes a week socializing with neighbours. For us, this is preferable. In other cultures, you may spend all your free time interacting with large, extended families.

People who have a low desire to spend time with friends, hanging out, talking, laughing, just being together, generally have more available hours in the week. This time can be spent honing your skills, something that makes you a better employee if that is what you want to do.

Having this Aspie neurology allows you to enter careers where you need to commit large amounts of time to the career, such as those jobs in the technology sector that require 60, 70, 80, or sometimes more hours a week. In one technology company, which shall remain unnamed, my husband worked alongside team-mates that stayed at the office nearly 24/7. The programmers would simply close their eyes, let their head rest, and 15 to 30 minutes later they would wake up and begin work again. There was no night; there was no day. They kept a change of clothes near their desk and changed every few days. They had breakfast in the break room. Lunch and dinner were delivered to the office. They left the office only rarely. They worked with only brief naps for respite. In this type of employment, there was room for no other interest.

We were fortunate in that Michael worked with this team for only three weeks. It was long enough for us to realize how much we appreciated how we had built a less work-intensive life.

While a non-stop workweek can easily be unhealthy, the opposite end is an employee who is easily distracted by a wide variety of social relationships. Many neurotypical employees may be less able to concentrate due to thoughts such as, "Oh, I wish I was hanging out with my large group of friends right now," or "My wife/friend/partner/children/parents are going to be angry if I don't call him/her/them during lunch," or "I think we should throw a party for ___ on Saturday. Who will we invite?"

An employee who is not so socially distracted has a distinct advantage over others.

There are probably very few Aspies who would be tempted by significant socialization with friends. This can make you a very focused employee. You can get the job done with fewer regrets.

CHAPTER 9

Your Position in the Company—Building It and Keeping It

In most work environments, there is a consistent flow of give and take between people. One person does one part of a project and you do another. There is a flow of reciprocal actions in the work environment. Understanding reciprocity, then dealing with it either directly or creatively, can be one of your best strategies at work. But first, a quick definition and description of social reciprocity and emotional reciprocity.

Social reciprocity may be a person saying "hello" after another has already extended a "hello." It may be giving a gift at Christmas. It may be any vocalization or action that expresses some sort of appropriate give and take.

Emotional reciprocity may be thanking a co-worker for his assistance. It may be expressing joy when a colleague expresses joy first, as in "My wife is having a baby!" or "I'm leaving on vacation tomorrow!" Emotional reciprocity may also be in the form of showing enthusiasm for your work when the boss expresses a desire for the team to be more enthusiastic.

A few examples of lack of reciprocity:

- Not expressing interest in a co-worker's conversation.

- Ignoring a co-worker's body language, facial expressions, or other nonverbal communications.

- Focusing so clearly on the task at hand that you do not engage in conversations.

While social and emotional reciprocity are key to building friendships and other peer relationships, there is a flip side to this coin. Lacking this ability can make you appear more like a manager or other superior.

Managers tend to not reciprocate fully. They cannot. When you fully reciprocate, you put yourself on a buddy–buddy level with the person you are talking to. Bosses need to maintain a broad viewpoint over all employees in order to stay objective.

Best Practice 22: Behaving Like
the Boss, i.e. Someone Well-Paid

Shocking but true—having an autistic brain can make you appear to be more "boss-like." Bosses are often distanced from their employees. Bosses can be rude and not have to worry as much about the consequences of that rudeness. Again, not fair, but unfortunately true.

The biggest pitfall you will have with your boss-like behavior is seeing only one side of the coin—the way that this behavior is a fault. Take a minute to look at the other side of the coin to see if recognizing this behavior can be good and beneficial to your career. If you can, channel this particular ability into successful career growth. One example follows.

Throughout Karly's career, her husband had encouraged her to be more friendly at work. Karly did not enjoy making friends at work. It only made things uncomfortable. She preferred keeping an emotional distance. Karly saw this as a personal fault and often felt badly about it, but did not change.

Mid-career, Karly read in a business book that people who want to "be the boss" do not buddy up with their colleagues. Future bosses focus on the projects, what needs to happen to help the company grow. Karly recognized her action of not building friendships as a positive and began to embrace the concept that she could be a great manager.

Within a few months, she was promoted and continued to hone her belief that being a bit distant was an asset. After she had achieved two advancements in a short time, Karly said, "I do not crave friendships the way other people do. This benefits me. I can focus on my work and be happy with where I am in life. I am my own best friend and that's plenty."

Aspies have the potential to be great managers, especially since it is easier for them to resist over-managing people on their team. A good leader generally hires good people then leaves them alone. In a non-AS manager's brain, he "trusts his team to make good choices." In an AS manager's brain, he "hired the right people and they already know what to do." He provides the framework then lets the team do their work. Within this context, social skills are not relevant—your strongest skill is your ability to leave people alone.

In my experience, people with AS have a uniquely strong ability to leave others alone. Very alone.

Another reason why a person with AS might be a better manager: A boss should not become best friends or even close friends with the person he is managing. People with non-AS brains often feel an inclination to bond with others. As someone with an AS brain, this desire is less intense and it allows you to stay on a boss–employee level more easily.

A common business saying is:

It is better to make a right decision than a popular one.

As an Aspie you have probably dealt with plenty of unpopular situations and lived through it. You are perhaps better suited than most to put up with resistance. Perhaps your ability to make tough, right decisions is a benefit, rather than a social deficit.

Best Practice 23: ASK for help—

The 42 Best Practices Notebook

If your goal is to focus on your strengths and minimize your weaknesses, then it makes sense to get help with the areas where you are weak. For example, if your executive function skills are lacking, then you may need to get assistance with organization, planning, and scheduling. (Please see earlier in this book) for a complete description of executive function.)

In my experience, the people I have known with AS have an *extremely* difficult time asking for help. My best guess is that it simply does not occur to them to ask. It is probably due to mindblindness, not realizing that others have solutions that you do not have. (Please see mindblindness explained previously.) Sometimes not asking for assistance in the areas where you most need help can make the issues become much bigger and more difficult.

In problematic situations, often those situations where asking for help is the best answer, you may feel like you have hit a brick wall.

When you hit a wall (when you have no solution to a difficult problem):

1. Identify the wall (example: so many papers on my desk that I cannot find the one I need).

2. Can I jump this wall myself? Do I want to jump this wall myself?

3. If yes, jump! If no, who can I ask for help?

Find a notebook you can use as your *42 Best Practices Notebook* and store it in a place you can easily refer to when needed. Write a list similar to the following. Customize it to fit your own needs and your own way of seeing the world, but do write it! It will help you more than you realize.

neighborhood girl $6 per week. The last time I spoke with Carrie she had received two pay raises over the span of less than one year, a fast advancement. Carrie was now earning $410 extra dollars each month.

This was a clear success. Note that it was not an obvious choice for a young single mother to hire a maid to do the dishes! Yet, unusual situations call for unusual solutions. It was crystal clear to Carrie and to those that knew Carrie that she was now experiencing a greater level of professional success. She credits that success to one single, simple strategy that helped her find a solution to one of her biggest, most annoying daily problems.

This strategy works not only with people with AS, but with people of all types who experience difficulties that shut down their brain function. You may call it a *Hitting the Wall* list or a main help sources list or whatever makes most sense to you, but whatever you do, *make the list.* At the time when you need it most, you will not have the cognitive ability to make it.

A personal example: In my early 20s, I suffered severe migraines. When the migraine hit, my mental functionality left me. I was no longer able to help myself. I would writhe in pain. That particular type of headache is called a suicide headache in the medical community—also known as a cluster headache—since patients do unfortunate things to be rid of the pain.

For years I was frustrated at the fact that there were so many ways for me to avoid the headaches, but the headache became a migraine and the migraine became a suicide headache before I could stop its progress. By the time I recognized I was about to lose mental function, it was already too late to think clearly enough to remember what I needed to do to get rid of the headache.

This experience was the nemesis for the first ever *Hitting the Wall* list. I wrote a list of 58 different tactics to avoid the headaches. The list included actions such as:

1. Drink a big glass of water (avoid dehydration).

2. Take the maximum dose of anti-inflammatory medicine.

3. Do a full set of yoga poses (a custom set of poses a friend had put together for me).

4. Ask a friend to do a shoulder and neck massage.

5. Drink a cup of chamomile tea.

6. Stop using the computer.

7. Clean something.

8. Wash my face with cold water.

9. Smile for five minutes.

10. Etc.

The success of this list was stunning. The list made it nearly impossible for the headache to advance to a full-blown suicide headache when I could cut it off with 58 different strategies for stopping the headache before it could intensify. It was my survival toolkit. You can make your own survival toolkit and, as any good scientist would do, test the effects of each one. As you refine your list, you may find an improvement spanning the breadth of your daily experience. The survival toolkit is described near the end of this book.

For this Best Practice, we merely started with the most important initial act—compiling a *Hitting the Wall/* main help sources list. Having such a list handy is a strategy that works for all types of people and all types of situations where the problem-solving part of the brain is no longer functional either temporarily or, as one man with autism said, "non-functional for unavoidably long-term purposes... The Out of Order sign is nailed down."

Best Practice 24: Brainspace

In my corner of the world, people often talk about "brainspace." The concept is that a person's brain has a limited amount of space. If you try to cram too much into that brainspace it becomes crowded and less functional. Another aspect is that you can give brainspace to a topic in order to consider it fully.

An example of a college student working a part-time job to support himself: Jim is often "fuzzy" with his brain and body so overloaded that he cannot remember to turn in assignments, go to work, or otherwise complete regular daily tasks.

The most successful solution for him so far has been the concept of brainspace. He has intense focus and, when he disrespects that focus by trying to split it, he loses the ability to take care of even the basics. Teaching how to split his attention would be useless, but helping him shift focus more fluidly has helped.

The highly visual concept of brainspace helped him see that he is allowing his entire brain to be overwhelmed by his failures, leaving no room to figure out the next steps he needs to take.

A specific example: One day after one of his classes, he skipped work so he could prepare for a test the next day. Sitting at his desk, all he could think of were the dozens of assignments in other classes that were sitting in his binder. When he was in class, all he could think of was how he needed to get to work as soon as classes dismissed.

Sitting at his desk obsessing over work did nothing but damage his already hurting brain. Once he arrived to work, he did the same thing—sit at his desk fretting over the overdue homework. I happened to see him sitting at his work desk, staring off into space, fidgeting and looking generally distressed.

I asked him what was bothering him and, once I had clarification, I said, "Jim, you have this much brainspace." With my finger, I drew a large circle on the top of his desk with my hand. "Right now this laptop full of work emails to answer and tasks to be completed is taking up your entire brainspace, right?" I placed his laptop directly in the middle of the circle.

He nodded and might have been pushing back tears. He looked very sad.

I moved his laptop to the side and said, "This does not need to be in your brainspace right now. It only hurts you to have it in your brainspace."

I moved the school binder full of late assignments into the center "brainspace" area and said, "This is the only thing that needs to be in your brainspace right now."

The transformation of his face was delightful. He had a goal in sight and his natural need to hyper-focus was now channeled properly.

Sometimes it can be just that simple.

A distracted employee costs money but gives little value in return. As a boss who is very conscious of the bottomline it was far more kind to both him and the company to let him have time off to work on his assignments and clear his mind so he could return to work the next day more prepared to focus on his job.

This approach works because it respects certain AS traits:

1. intense focus

2. sensory overload

3. visual models.

The brainspace concept can be applied nicely to a work environment, particularly one where the person with AS has a desk.

Desks quickly become overloaded with papers going in, going out, papers that need to be filed, ones that need immediate action, and ones that need to be thrown away or shredded. The brainspace concept works by drawing a mental circle in the center of the desk and, while working on that one specific thing, ignoring everything else.

Recognizing the brainspace concept is a powerful tool in helping you self-protect against overload on the job. Often, too many tasks will come at you all at once. Since you have a hyper-focused brain, seeing too many To Dos at once can be overwhelming. You may end up "frozen," not able to accomplish any task because you have no idea where to begin. You can avoid this by making sure you recognize and protect the way your own brain works.

Focus on one thing at a time; ignore the rest. If you find this works for you, it may help create more relaxing, productive days for you. If you find that your boss, co-workers, employees, etc.

can respect your need for hyper-focused brainspace, then you have wonderful odds for professional success.

Best Practice 25: Securing
Your Job and Scoring a Raise

Out of all the aspects of having an autistic brain, the inclination to not spontaneously share your achievements with others is most detrimental to your financial success.

It is also the most difficult.

Pay raises are supposed to be given based on an employee's contribution to the company. But in actuality, pay raises are based on the amount you appear to have contributed.
The perception of your contribution will be based partly on actual fact and partly on your ability to impress.

Here are three potential methods for communicating your value to the team:

1. visual appearance

2. written confirmation

3. results.

We will discuss the specifics of these top three methods, but first let's look at why these may take a significant, conscious effort on your part.

Why will your boss know the extent of your contribution if you do not communicate it to him? Mindblindness, even if you have only a small bit of it, may cause you to think that your boss already knows about your accomplishments. This is a dangerous assumption, dangerous for your paycheck.

First example: Henry was a shy engineer who never bragged about his successes. One colleague called him "The Anti-Bragger" of their division. When asked what he had accomplished, Henry always minimized his work. For example, if he had completed a full set of testing, he would say that he "did a little" testing.

To make it worse, during the yearly employee review, as Henry was being complimented on one of his accomplishments, he actually denied part of it. While he received the normal pay raise increase for that year, his Christmas bonus was reduced due to his report of underachievement.

Henry's minimizing his successes was a coping strategy he had learned as a child. Henry was hyperlexic, i.e. he began reading at a very early age. Often adults would give inappropriately enthusiastic amounts of attention to him for his early reading, gushing over him: "Oh! Henry is so smart!" and "Henry, read this encyclopedia entry for us. Show everybody what you can do!" People did the same with math facts, requiring him to perform during dinner parties and other on-the-spot occasions: "Henry, tell everyone what 385 times 17 equals!"

As a survival strategy, Henry learned the many ways he could minimize the level of attention and accolades he received for his accomplishments.

This was an appropriate strategy when he was a child, but it undermined him on the job. He was being paid far less than he was worth because he did not see how he needed to advocate for himself.

Second example: During one of Michael's interviews, we practiced for several hours before the interview. It was a job that Michael wanted badly. So, we scripted many potential answers to questions.

When Michael came home from the interview, it was obvious that he was in full sensory overload. For Michael, overload often appears as a physical exhaustion so intense that it looks like he is asleep while standing. His breathing is deathly slow and shallow. His posture is hunched and deflated. His eyes are barely open and all of his muscles, including those in his face, are stone-still. In these situations, if I were to ask "Tell me how it went," I would have received no reply. Instead I asked "What was said?" so he could repeat back chunks of the conversation exactly as they occurred, thus using the AS tendency to "parrot," repeating back conversation as it occurred originally.

Terry worked at a software company in the 90s. Every software project had a credits page that listed the people who had worked on the software package, usually 20 people. The first software project Terry worked on listed everyone except her. The technical writer had missed quiet Terry when writing the credits list.

Terry said nothing about the omission of her name and was not surprised to see her name omitted from the next project too. This time Terry asked her boss why. Her boss said, "Oh, I'll ask the technical writer. I don't know why." On the third project Terry's name was included.

At this point in Terry's career, she had enough background with the team and enough job security to ask her boss for flextime. She spent 90 percent of her time working from her home office. She only came in to the office for short meetings once every few weeks.

On the fourth software release, Terry's name was omitted from the credits list. Terry consoled herself by saying that it was "not a big deal."

Unfortunately, the flextime arrangement did not work out. Terry was fired for "not completing the tasks assigned to her." The tasks were completed—by her—but a colleague was claiming credit for them. Since Terry was not there to see the inaccuracy, she was not able to correct it. By the time she discovered the misunderstanding, the boss and the entire team all believed that Terry had been slacking for months.

After being fired, Terry took a few weeks off work to deal with the anger she felt over the situation. When she started job hunting, she listed on her resume the projects she had contributed to, but when recruiters verified her resume, they did not find her name on the credits lists of the projects she claimed to have worked on.

Terry had an extremely difficult job search and finally took a job well below her previous pay level.

Best Practice 26: Motivation Matters

For those of you with AS who would only consider work in an area that you are personally interested in, I will let you in on a little secret from the neurotypical world—many people work only for the money. They are motivated by survival, their ability to pay for shelter, food, and clothing.

While you might be similarly motivated, there is a good chance that your preference is to do a particular job that is linked to a particular interest and it is solely your personal desire to do it. The pay is an added bonus. One prime example of this type of motivation is found in the technology sector, in Linux development in particular. (A description of Linux was included in a previous section)

In free and open software development, people do work for the fun of it, work that normally would be high-paid labor. At sites like http://code.google.com or http://sourceforge.net or http:s// launchpad.net people volunteer, particularly those with an intense love of programming, documenting, testing, designing, and other tasks needed in the tech sector.

Here is your AS strength: When you are motivated by the task itself, you have a much higher chance of success. When you care about the actual project being produced, that is your end goal. You are far more likely to produce a quality product, to resist cutting corners, and to truly care about what you have made.

Here is a quick comparison of what happens during the difficult phases of a project (and every project has difficult phases) when we are motivated by ends other than the task itself.

1. Motivated by money

If the company/team/project goes through tight times, when funds are limited (and every company/team/project goes through tight times) the person motivated by money is significantly de-motivated, and quality of work suffers. This person will seek to increase personal gain before seeking the success of the project.

Sometimes more personal gain is to be had by delaying the project or limiting the project's success. For example, if employees are paid extra for overtime, the money-motivated employees will be tempted to work slowly, thus more easily justifying their need to work overtime. This is bad.

2. Motivated by attention

If there are personality conflicts on the team—if a more dominant player/employee enters the team—the person motivated by attention is de-motivated and work suffers. This person will do things to attract attention again, whether or not they contribute to the success of the project.

On many projects, the end goal is best reached by people keeping focused on their own tasks. For people motivated by attention, they will distract others so they can get another minute or two of attention. They will cause scenes in meetings to get lots of attention all at once. Their main goal is to have the other's time and attention shifted towards them, not the project. This is bad.

3. Motivated by power

This person will seek more personal power whether or not it contributes to the success of the project. While many managers are motivated by power, there are also plenty of employees who are similarly motivated. They seek control, power, and authority whether it is rightly theirs or not.

Sometimes, but not often, a person will receive more power if the project is not successful. For example, a manager will be given more employees if the project seems to need more staff to get it done. An even more destructive scenario is, when a restructuring occurs (restructuring happens often in many industries), the person who is motivated by power will do whatever it takes to wiggle into positions of greater power whether or not they are qualified to fulfill the job responsibilities of the new, more powerful position.

I have never seen any of the above happen with a person with AS. In fact, I have seen the opposite. There is even an official term for it: The halo effect. Read on.

Best Practice 27: The Halo Effect—Avoid It

There are many people in the world who select their job based on what society says they should do. A boy who is good with numbers may be prompted to become a statistician or a mathematics professor. A girl with AS who loves creating her own science experiments, writing down the results meticulously, and performing the experiment again and again until she has figured out all the factors may be prompted to become a scientist.

But the problem is that we often do not pay close attention to the details of the restricted interest. Often the interests are quite restricted: the girl might be only interested in performing experiments with sand and dirt. Perhaps as she develops her career, she will see that she dislikes 90 percent of the things she does as a scientist and lose sight of her original, true love. If she can remember what makes her happy, she can get the training she needs; then she can search for a career in material sciences where she can do as many experiments as she likes with sand and dirt from all over the world.

For example, one scientist with a similar background is currently going on expeditions over the Antarctic, drilling for samples of the Earth in the most unaltered form. Her planes leave from a little island off the South Island, New Zealand. These core samples are her life's goal. There is no topic, no activity, nothing more interesting to her than her work.

It is not inherently bad to be very interested in one particular subject. These spikes in interest are powerful talents.

Unfortunately sometimes misperceptions can cause problems.

In the Halo Effect...and Eight Other Business Delusions that Deceive Managers, Phil Rosenzweig (2009) explains a difficult situation that occurs when a person is so brilliant on the job that people assume he is brilliant with everything he does. It is a generalization that may or may not be accurate.

The halo effect is the belief that, if someone has one particularly beneficial trait, they have beneficial traits in every area of being. The first tests that proved the halo effect were tests showing that people generally believed beautiful people to be more intelligent— even though there was no evidence of that superior intelligence.

The halo effect happens in the work environment too. When you have one particularly strong ability, people may begin to believe that you have strengths in all areas. While this may be flattering, the consequences can be quite unpleasant. For example, if you show excellent skill in your current position, you may be advanced to the next highest position whether you are qualified for it or not.

To give this concept greater context, let's look at Michael, my own husband, who has experienced the halo effect year after year in his various positions as programmer.

Michael is a great programmer, so skilled that he has often been given the title of lead programmer, indicating management of other people. The title senior engineer is far more appropriate since it involves no management other than technical expertise.

This difficulty happened because, whenever anyone had a problem, they knew that Michael could fix it. Even in his early years, when he was still young and inexperienced, his colleagues quickly noticed that he could solve problems no one else could due to his calm hyper-focus on the problem exclusively.

At one job, the president of the company had a problem that no one else on staff could help him with. The company employed several hundred people and this president had tasked many different experts to solve it. No one could figure it out. He heard from one manager that there was an entry-level employee who could "solve anything."

The president took the elevator down to the floor where Michael worked, walked through the maze of cubicles until he found the young, inexperienced coder. He introduced himself to Michael, pulled up a chair, and showed Michael the problem. Michael looked at it and within only a few minutes of quietly staring at the problem Michael pointed to the one part of the problem that needed to be fixed, explained the solution, and turned back to his computer.

The president later wrote a letter of thanks to Michael that Michael still has to this day. He was proud that he was able to solve problems that no one else could. This was a fantastic fulfillment of the top two levels of the Maslow for Aspies Pyramid of Need. Michael was presented with a challenging project (the top level) and he received recognition and prestige in return (the second-to-top level).

So, what does the president do when he identifies such a brilliant employee? He promotes that employee to the highest level of responsibility that seems appropriate for that employee regardless of that employee's full scope of ability.

For a programmer going into a full management position, this can be a recipe for disaster. For a research scientist going into managing a team of researchers, it can guarantee that the project will never reach a final completion date. For an accountant who has a brilliant ability to spot patterns of irregularity in tax records, being promoted to managing other accountants can lead to an unpleasant resistance that makes it hard for that "formally brilliant" accountant to be motivated to go to work the next day.

In Michael's career field, and the careers of many other Aspies, being promoted means taking on management tasks. Michael was not a good manager nor did he want to become a good manager. He just wanted to be left alone to write good code.

The halo effect has happened to Michael repeatedly in every job he has held. During one job transition, he was offered a job in another state. Together we traveled to the new state to see if it was a good move for our family. During dinner with the company owner, Darrel, a few things became apparent that Michael had not noticed.

Darrel was hiring Michael as a *manager*, not as a programmer. Darrel had heard that Michael was "the best programmer on the west coast" and figured that was who he wanted leading the team. Unfortunately during the interview, Michael's distaste for management-type interactions was not apparent.

From day one at that particular job, Michael avoided the management tasks. The people around him took care of the tasks that were not getting done and slowly a different colleague took on the management tasks that were supposed to be Michael's responsibility. Soon that person became the manager in title also.

This happened with the next job and the next.

Beware of the halo effect. In your interviews and meetings with your boss, make it clear what your talents are. If you state it in a positive way, you will help the manager have a clear view of your future with the company.

If you state it in a negative way, your manager will see you as unworkable, unwilling to grow, and resisting tasks even before being asked to do them. A few Do Not Use examples of how you might word it negatively by mistake:

> "I am not good at managing people so I would prefer to stay in my position as ___."

or

> "I am hoping that you will never promote me. I don't want to move from the job I currently have."

or (which is unfortunately a real example)

> "I hate managing. I was fired for being a screw-up manager at my last job."

Note that the Do Not Use sentences involve negatives: "not good" and "never," "don't," "hate," "fired," and "screw-up."

Here are a couple of examples of how you can spin a negative as a positive, valuable trait:

> "My greatest skill is ___ which is what I am currently doing. Throughout the years I will be your most reliable and motivated employee with these tasks."

or

"I have been reading a book about management that deals with people specifically like me and my work style (this book). It suggests that perhaps the greatest, most fulfilling career path for me would be to continue doing what I'm currently doing for as long as I possibly can. If you can allow me the freedom to not advance, even though it keeps my pay scale at this level, I will be one of your most valuable employees. Would that work for you and this department?"

Conversations like these are difficult and are best practiced ahead of time, scripted and rehearsed until you are comfortable and confident.

That said, for many people with AS, no matter how hard you practice, the conversation probably will be unpleasant.

1. *Filing a DE-34 with the federal government.* (Probably all industrial countries have some sort of paperwork that needs to be filed when an employee is hired.) Paperwork takes time, usually the bookkeeper's or accountant's time. Their time is expensive.

2. *A new set of everything for that new employee:* Perhaps a new desk (at least a cleaned-off one from the previous employee), new supplies, a new employee manual, new or cleaned/wiped computer, etc.

3. *Training:* Possibly the most expensive part of hiring a new employee is the long and tedious training process. Some employees learn quickly, but more often than not, training takes longer and is less effective than anticipated.

4. *What an employer wants most of all is an employee who can be hired, trained, do a good job, and stay.* Another reason, US-specific, but perhaps common in other countries: Every time I fire someone from my company, it raises my company's tax rate. At the time of this writing new employers have the set rate of 3.4% for the first year. This means that for every $100,000 they pay their employees, $3400 of additional money needs to go to the government. The government then funnels this money to unemployment so that, when people are laid off, the government can help them with basic living expenses until they find their next job.

   If I can retain my employees and not have too many firings, my tax rate slowly decreases and my company will get to keep more of its hard-earned money. There is very direct fiscal compensation for keeping employees long-term.

   It is highly beneficial to a company's bottomline to hire people who are stable. The most stable people I know are people with autism. One example: Ned, a friend of mine, is a researcher at a local university. When he started college, he knew he wanted to stay in college as long as he would. He ended up getting his PhD. Instead of getting a job in industry, he found a job at the university that he had just graduated from.

He will never move from his job unless forced to do so. He will still be a researcher at this university until the day he retires. Once he retires, he will probably continue to go to university campus every day, probably in a volunteer position.

In his words, he "doesn't want to ever move" and he wants to "keep doing what [he] is doing" for the rest of his life.

Ned is one of the most stable employees I have ever met. He is every boss's dream employee since he does a superb job, knowing that he needs to be the best and brightest in order to stay relevant in his position. He will never be distracted by other job opportunities; his devotion and loyalty will never be split.

My goal as an employer is to find as many Neds as I can and hire them as fast as I can.

Best Practice 29: Loyalty

I learned a personal lesson about loyalty from my husband. Once, when we were having a horrible argument, I threw off my wedding ring and said, "It's over!"

He would not take off his and I asked why. He could not answer, but later I learned that he keeps his wedding ring on half out of love for me and half out of love for stability.

Compare his ability to stay married to a person without this particular "inflexibility" trait. If you used points to rank loyalty, a comparison might look like this:

Steve: 80 points for loving his wife
When times are tough, those 80 points are quickly depleted and his loyalty point balance goes negative. Separation and divorce occur.

Timothy: 80 points for loving his wife + 80 points for not wanting to change the current structure of his life

When times are tough, Timothy can lose all love for his wife and there are still 80 more solid, hard-to-lose points that keep his wedding ring on his finger.

Note that there are plenty of people without AS that stay married out of apathy, but I am not talking about laziness. In the person with AS, when they married, they made a choice to partner with a particular person and that partnership was permanent in their mind. This can be seen as devotion, loyalty, stability, and all sorts of other wonderful traits that are often found sorely lacking in others.

This love-of-stability is prevalent over all areas of life. In the office Timothy's work will stay stable while Steve's becomes erratic as he deals with divorce. Timothy is also more likely to stay devoted to the company because he has +80 enjoyment from his job plus +80 enjoyment of the stability of the job.

Best Practice 30: Trust

I wish there was a way to shout this one from the mountaintops to other employers: "Want an employee you can trust? Hire an Aspie!!"

Aspies are often said to be cursed with honesty. What a wonderful, valuable trait for a person to have on their team.

A smart employer will recognize the tremendous value of having someone with AS on any given team. That team member, especially if known for his or her honesty, can help keep the team on track.

One example: In a small warehouse, Howard worked assembling various consumer electronic devices. During the pre-Christmas rush one season, Howard overheard one of the employees next to him talking about how they could take a few items from inventory then change the total number recorded in the computer's inventory system so no one would notice they had been taken.

Howard had learned from tough experiences previously that it is always better to talk to the teacher or boss before the problem happens rather than after, even if it might be perceived as tattling.

The next morning Howard knocked on his boss's door. Howard's boss, James, listened carefully as Howard described what he had overheard the night before. James was quick to act and immediately called all employees in for a meeting.

During the meeting, James carefully detailed that the company's inventory and their security had been tested recently (a white lie, but efficient in its purpose) and that it was especially important to remember to count inventory carefully this year because "all mistakes will be caught and taken out of your paycheck if you were the one on duty when it happened."

James was able to quickly deter any potential theft thanks to the open honesty Howard shared. Howard was now the most valuable employee his boss had. After the Christmas rush, the employee who had considered theft was let go. James asked Howard to sit in during interviews when hiring the new staff. This was ideal for Howard since he was able to select a new co-worker who was the most likely to be a good co-worker for him in particular.

Best Practice 31: Keeping the Machine Running

A person with a usually strong adherence to routine can be one of the most valuable employees a manager can have. He or she can also be one of the best managers a company can have.

Within any company, there are managers and employees who have to do tasks that are mundane, routine, and generally boring. People without autism may have a very hard time accomplishing tasks that are too routinized.

Let's look at one example of this trait in practice. This is only one small, specific example. The ways this trait can be an asset on the job are numerous. It can make you a highly valuable, highly reliable person.

In most companies that develop software, there are many software developers working with a body of code at any given time. In order to work on the code without messing each other up, they "check out" the code the same way you would check out a book from the library.

rates based on www.monster.com and http://salary.com rates as of June 2010.)

One field wherein many Aspies are quite happy—universities. At Stanford, a university close to where I live, professors earn between $150,000 and $275,000/year based on the particular department they have chosen as their specialty. (Salary rates based on the "Stanford Faculty Staff Information" fact sheet published by the Office of the Provost.)

These salaries are quite generous, especially considering that the average salary in the USA tends to be around $40,000/year. (Based on www.worldsalaries.org.)

"Stereotyped and repetitive motor mannerisms" do not necessarily ban you from the possibility of working in a job that can provide fiscal comfort.

But before we continue this section, let's note that there are some body movements that are so extreme that they make co-workers uncomfortable. It would be naive to state that you can get a great job no matter what your particular set of body movements entails.

Best Practice 33: Building Support

If you do have large body movements that co-workers and bosses would find uncomfortable (and then make work more difficult for you) there are several options. This is assuming that you have already tried all potential medical treatments, occupational therapy, and other methods to reduce the negative impact of the movements.

First, consider having an open and honest talk with your colleagues. A potential conversation could go like this:

> "_____ (name of boss or co-worker), can I ask you about something? I know that I make odd movements sometimes. I'm really sorry about that. I have already tried getting it to calm down. It's worst when I am stressed. It is actually my body's way of calming itself down naturally. It helps me stay calm and focused. Is there any way you can overlook it?"

This is only a sample script. It contains all the elements you need to gain your co-worker's support. Let's break it down so you can see the necessary elements clearly.

1. "_____ (name of boss or co-worker)" Call the person by name in order to get his focused attention. If it is a group of people, replace the personalized greeting with a casual "Hi…" or "Hey guys…"

2. "…Can I ask you about something?…" People often lead into a conversation by asking permission to talk. This step seems to be skipped often and I am not sure why. It is perhaps based in the "lack of social reciprocity" or the mindblindness of AS, but in most conversations, it is best to have a lead-in that helps the person you are talking to feel more comfortable responding to you. Consider it the snow shovel of the conversation. If the conversation is a walk down a snowy street, your front bumper, the "…Can I ask you about something?…" is the snow shovel that initially pushes the snow out of the way, making possible for you and your co-worker to walk down this path.

3. "…I know that I make odd movements sometimes…" Address the issue directly. You may want to say the specific movement, such as "I seem to throw my arm back for no apparent reason." Do not actually make the motion when describing it! If the motion is significant enough to mention, it is probably a motion that makes people uncomfortable. The purpose of this conversation is to make the co-worker comfortable with you, not emphasize the problem. If you can, avoid making the motion. The co-worker is probably already aware of what you are talking about.

4. "…I'm really sorry about that…" This is an acknowledgement that you know the motion makes people uncomfortable and that you wish it was easier. People are usually much more receptive when you openly admit fault. Please do not

Best Practice 34: Channeling
Sensory Needs into Career Needs

If you have "repetitive motor mannerisms" this section will benefit you.

A few examples of what these motor mannerisms may look like from my set of acquaintances:

- odd hand gestures that involve what looks like pointing at random things
- shoulder twitching
- neck cracking
- leg twitching
- a bounciness to a person's movements in general
- head going back and forth the way a chicken's head moves while walking
- head tilted at a sharp angle to one side whenever someone is talking nearby
- hitting leg with hands in fists
- and the classic—hand flapping.

There are many, many more. These mannerisms are as various as the human race itself. The defining factor is that they are repetitive and odd. Whatever defines "odd" I will never know, other than it is a societal judgement.

There is a chance that you can channel the sensory need into part of your chosen profession. I will give examples of one odd trait below.

One man with autism, Sam, had hand flapping as a child. He was severely reprimanded for it by his father. He learned to hide the flapping, but the sensory need morphed into an odd finger pointing that he could not resist doing while talking. The way Sam avoided more severe reprimanding from his father was simply by not talking around his father.

As an adult, Sam could not be so silent at work and in public. He generally let the pointing occur and did not expend too much effort to stop it. He often thought, "It isn't that odd. Who cares anyway?" The pointing only occurs when he is talking about something he is very interested in. It is not completely normal, but it is not too terribly odd either. No one takes too much notice of it.

But, here is how he managed to control the sensory need: He learned how to type and as a teenager he spent significant time at a keyboard. As an adult, he often has several laptops in his backpack. (The weight of the backpack feels good to him.) At work he often spends 10 to 12 hours a day on a keyboard, receiving the sensory feedback his hands seem to need.

Sam was able to morph an unacceptable movement into a movement that was more of a part of his personality than an oddity.

Another example is of a man with AS who experienced similar hand flapping as a child. As a teenager, he tried hard to keep the flapping under control, but it was difficult. When Ted was 12 he had a teacher who was always writing on the board during lectures. The teacher used his hands constantly: pointing, waving, writing in a flappy type of way, but it was a useful way as the professor explained various equations on the chalkboard.

Ted made the connection that, if he became a math teacher when he grew up, he would get to flap his hands around and people would think he was a smart, brilliant, energetic teacher while he got all the flapping he wanted. Ted became dedicated to achieving the goal of being a teacher someday.

Today, while Ted is not a math teacher, he is a professor in engineering at a prestigious university. His lectures are filled with energy and enthusiasm as he uses his laptop to project the lecture notes, graphs, and charts onto the large projection screen at the front of the classroom.

Ted is quite happy in his personal and professional life and privately he credits a large part of his personal success to finding a way he can incorporate a "repetitive hand motion" that he finds calming into his everyday life.

Ted's diagnostic "syndrome" is what makes him the brilliantly energetic teacher he is.

CHAPTER 12

Unique Aspie Preoccupations on the Job

As a child, you may have taken apart various things around the house in order to see how they worked. If that was not allowed, perhaps you tinkered with things that were already in "parts." This type of preference, while seemingly innocuous, is quite telling in what type of career this person with AS will fit best.

For example, let's detail my job as CEO and my husband's job.

As a non-Aspie CEO, I must look at the entire scope of the company. I need to evaluate how the company is performing internally (Are tasks getting done? Are the employees happy?) as well as the company's position in the world at large (Are any competitors getting too close? How can I differentiate our company for the long haul?). I need to look at how we have performed in the past and how we can perform better in the future. This type of work is the opposite of "focus."

My husband with AS focuses intensely on one project at a time, giving it such deep thought that he often stays up until the wee hours of the morning completing one single process that is so deep and so complex that most people could not possibly come close to solving it. In a recent example, he was working hard to solve a problem and in the end, once solved, he expressed, "Even the manufacturers of this product would not have been able to solve this problem. Obviously They didn't solve this problem!"

When my husband and I talk about work, it is far too easy to see the wrong side of the coin with each other's talents and skills. I am tempted to see him as having an "inability to see the big picture." He may be tempted to say that I am "not as intelligent" as him due to my inability to dive into the more difficult, deeper concepts. I am very lucky that he does not express this sentiment.

In the work environment, this difference will be exacerbated.

Best Practice 35: The Manager and the Builder

In order to work well in your chosen career, it is important to recognize that it takes many various talents to build a company. In any job, whether as a retail clerk, a lawyer, a programmer, or an engineer, you need the talents of others and they need your talents too. Keeping this solidly in mind will significantly help you as a team member. Why?

You may think that your personal, private thoughts about someone are exactly that—personal and private. Yet they are not. Unfortunately we unknowingly give clues as to how we honestly feel about people, usually in facial expressions (preferably in microexpressions—the ones that last only a millisecond and can only be overtly detected by a small number of people). We also unwittingly communicate our true feelings about someone through body language, through the words we use, and through the assumptions we make.

For example, if a computer programmer believes his boss is an idiot, he will be hesitant to explain things in detail and will instead make important decisions without consulting his boss. If that boss believes his programmers are idiots, he will be more inclined to make unilateral decisions without their input.

If your thoughts for each other are positive, you are more likely to collaborate and work together successfully.

To illustrate, let's look at Mike and Aaron. Aaron has AS and Mike does not. Mike is a popular manager who often has parties at his home on the weekends. Since Aaron does not come to the

squeezing in phone calls, in-person visits, and many other meetings. In contrast, makers (most likely people with AS) do their work by intensely focusing on a project for long periods of time. Managers tend to interrupt makers. Help your manager see that your way of doing things is valid and that the interruptions not only decrease the quality of work, but can be actually painful.

2. In return, respect your manager's way of doing things by trying to make yourself available and interruptible when possible. To support this second point, the following experience shows one man's way of making interruptions far less unpleasant.

One man with AS, Billy, has struggled for years trying to remember to pull out of his preoccupation long enough and often enough to take care of himself. Many people with AS have the same experience Billy does—forgetting to eat, drink, or even go to the bathroom while engrossed in his particularly well-loved interest. His body suppresses signals of hunger, fatigue, thirst, and other basic survival needs.

Billy's advice: "I surround myself with interruptions." He chooses to work near others rather than working in a quiet spot. The time of day when he has the most problems is after his wife and children have gone to bed. When the distractions are minimized, he gets so lost in his work that he often forgets to go to bed until early morning. This starts a cycle where he works at night and sleeps during the day. Sleeping at work is a surefire way to lose your job. To top it off, his wife believes he is doing it on purpose, "...you are avoiding me. You don't love me...," and the children see that their father would rather sleep than play with them: "Daddy, you like sleep more than me."

Now that Billy is aware of the repercussions of his tendency to be fully immersed at night, he asks his wife to "entice him" to go to bed at a good time and, not surprisingly, it works!

While this is only one particular solution for one particular person, the general rule is: If you have a preoccupation that is causing a detrimental disappearing act on your part, perhaps introducing some simple distractions will be the best solution.

One more benefit: If the distractions in your office, your home, and your life in general are feeling too unwanted, too pressing, and too awful, perhaps you can find solace in the simple thought that these distractions can serve a useful purpose in certain situations.

Best Practice 36: Neurotypical
Meetings and Aspie Survival

In 2004 Patrick Lencioni wrote a book titled *Death by Meeting: A Leadership Fable...About Solving the Most Painful Problem in Business* wherein Lencioni expressed how the meetings we have at work (the highly social get-togethers) can destroy productivity and employee morale. He advocates a far more efficient structure for company meetings. Nearly every person I spoke to in the technical sector about the book raved about the theories and new best practices.

Perhaps fittingly, the people I spoke to in less technical, more managerial, more socially oriented careers were less excited about the concepts in *Death by Meeting*. I felt this showed an interesting ulterior motive to having meetings—some people enjoyed meetings simply to get together and interact socially, not to further the end goals of the team, the project, or the company.

Talk doesn't cook rice.—ancient Chinese Proverb

As the world becomes more efficient and less tolerant of waste, the social get-togethers will become less acceptable to upper management, especially financial managers who are looking at the overall efficiency of their departments. When they see the lack of efficiency of managers suffocating productivity by get-togethers under the guise of official meetings, those will be the first to be chopped during financially tight times.

The easiest advice is for how to survive meeting—stay relatively quiet. It is harder to get in trouble for silence than it is for saying the wrong thing.

Another useful rule: *Praise in public; criticize in private.* When you have a criticism for someone you work with, especially if it is your boss, do not express the criticism during a meeting. If you need to communicate something negative, do it in private, between just you and the person who is receiving the criticism.

During a meeting, if you do offer input, give positive suggestions. If you cannot find a way to give a positive suggestion, try to do some quick coin flipping in your head. For example:

Example 1:
"I think that project suggestion is a rotten idea" can be flipped to:

"It sounds like we are making progress. Let's keep considering more ideas."

Example 2:
"This is the worst idea I have ever heard" can be flipped to:

"We have had so many great ideas in the past." (In your mind, this makes sense—if this is the worst idea then previous ideas have been better.)

Example 3:
"You are wrong" can be flipped to:

"I am not sure I am understanding what you are saying. Can you explain it again?" Often people realize their own errors when they have a chance to think about what they said a little more. This may not always be the case, but it is worth a try.

Example 4:
"Can I go now? This has been the most boring meeting of my life and I would rather not waste any more time on it" can be flipped to:

"Oh, guys, sorry but I just remembered I need to finish ____ (name of project) before five tonight..."

Example 5:
"The deadline for this project is insane" can be flipped to:

"Can we look a little more closely at the tasks that need to be done? It looks like we might be underestimating the effort needed to complete this project to the level of quality we need."

Example 6:
"I can't believe you made such a stupid mistake" can be flipped to:

"Our team is usually so careful... Can we look at how this mistake happened so we can make sure it doesn't happen again?"

Example 7:
"You didn't give me enough instructions/resources/background to get this job done" can be flipped to:

"Thank you for having such a high opinion of me! But I actually need more information to finish this project. Thanks."

Example 8:
"You guys really shouldn't make me do all your work for you" can be flipped to:

"I am so glad that you all trust me to do great work to complete a large chunk of this project, but I am working so much overtime that the quality of my work is going to deteriorate unless we can find a way to balance the work a little better."

Example 9:
"It's too loud in here! Please shut up!" can be flipped to:

"I appreciate that you are all so enthusiastic about this project, but we need a level of calm if we are going to get anything done."

Example 10:
"Why did you make this decision without me? That was stupid since I'm the one who will make this project happen" can be flipped to:

"It looks like this decision has already been made. But, would you consider some input from me? I have information that you may not have considered yet."

When saying something negative, reprimanding, or otherwise criticizing, point out only the specifics. Do not make any sweeping generalizations. Do not mention anything irrelevant (other than potential positive aspects). The person you are speaking to may be at the end of a long list of problems, but only discuss the ones that pertain to getting the work done. The rest is irrelevant.

To sum up, the 42 Best Practices advice for surviving meetings is to:

1. Stay relatively quiet to avoid as many problems as possible.

2. In every comment you make, ensure it is positive and solution-based. If it is a negative comment, flip it before you say it.

3. Detox afterwards. Find a way to calm down after the meeting. There is a good chance that the meeting, since it involves a quick-firing mesh of social interactions, will be stressful.

This last step is important because it helps you survive future meetings better. If you fail to take this last step, your body will begin to register the message:

Meeting → *sensory overload* → *pain* which lasts a long, long time, compounding into the next difficult situation you face that day.

The next time you have to attend a meeting, the anxiety will be more obvious. Anxiety builds as your body dreads the after-effect, creating a cyclical, escalating pattern.

If you take the last step outlined above, you can encode the following into your body's reaction to meetings:

Meeting → *sensory overload* → *detox*, at which point your body realizes that the overload lasts only a short time.

Do not expect meetings to be fun, but do expect them to be survivable.

Best Practice 37: Well-Rounded Is
Not the Goal—Let Your Freak Flag Fly

This is perhaps my favorite part of the diagnostic criteria to explore because turning it upside down can be invigorating to those who are accustomed to a life of rejection and negative labels.

Looking from a viewpoint of sickness, how could difficulties in such wide-sweeping areas of your life lead to a successful strategy for your work environment? How could a "clinically significant impairment" be good for your career?

1. The diagnosis for AS was written from a viewpoint of sickness.

2. Some careers require sickness!

In the book *Lucky or Smart: Fifty Pages for the First-Time Entrepreneur* Bo Peabody (2008) expresses that many people who start companies are mentally imbalanced; they have to be! In order to work the crazy hours, experience non-stop problems, and deal with untold amounts of stress, you have to be a bit mentally disabled. If you had a balanced sense of working eight hours a day then getting a good night's sleep, you would never make it through the first week of a start-up company. And in order to see a start-up through to success, you have to be semi-insane to purposefully put yourself through the anxiety, overwork, and heartache of a long-term schedule.

Yet, start-up entrepreneurs are seen kindly in the world's view.

Why can't people with AS, also a mental impairment, be seen as similarly skilled and talented?

Perhaps the following phrase will carry through to a solution on a problem or two: *Use your impairments to empower your work.*

It is as simple as that, or at least it can be. I recently heard a man with high-functioning autism (relatively similar to AS) expressing, "I would love to be a systems administrator, but I am autistic [AS]." While there are most definitely limitations integrated into the AS brain, those limitations do not necessarily prohibit your ability to express your talents in meaningful ways.

For a moment, take a step back from the diagnostic criteria and look at humanity in general.

What are a few names of famous people? Are they particularly well-rounded people?

It is most likely that the famous people you remember were actually quite imbalanced in their lives. They were far more interesting and note-worthy than the "well-balanced" people with smooth social skills.

You may be tempted to admire or even covet the traits that well-rounded people seem to hold. I have fallen into this trap many times, looking at successful women who seem to "have it all." Time after time, when I find out more about that person's life, I realize that I would not trade places with her. My structure of my life and the shape of my character are my own.

Many companies are starting to recognize how important it is to respect and nuture unique talent. To provide a bit of anecdotal context for this point, let's look at what the more prestigious US universities are seeking for this year's incoming student population (who in four to eight years will be employees and employers).

Recently there were several meetings on my oldest son's high school campus where college recruiters would visit the high school to encourage students to apply to their university. My son's high school, Berkeley High, is a large, diverse, rigorous high school. With 3400 students in attendance it is a large student body and the universities would love to entice the best and the brightest to apply for admission to their university.

The main college preparation event had five different recruiters from five different prestigious universities who were all trying to encourage students to apply. Each recruiter had ten minutes to present their school.

The first recruiter that stood up was from Stanford University, one of the most prestigious universities on the west coast of the US. He was a tremendous hulk of a man, standing at 6 feet 11 inches tall, African American with rippling muscles and a smile as wide as could be. He was not the stereotypical "man of academia."

He stood up, gave a brief introduction, then, with a large gesture, threw his arms open and boomed, "We are seeking imbalanced students."

It sent a little electrical wave through the audience and the recruiter went on to explain that students who were well-balanced, with near-perfect scores in nearly every area, who were thus skilled in nearly every area, were some of the most boring students a university could have. Yes, these achievers would most likely have successful well-paid careers, but Stanford was seeking "shooting stars."

Some of Stanford's previous students include Sergey Brin and Lawrence Page, the founders of Google; Doris Fisher, co-founder of Gap; Reed Hastings, Chairman and CEO of Netflix; William Hewlett and David Packard, founders of HP; Philip Knight, Chairman and CEO of Nike; Scott McNealy, Chairman of Sun Microsystems; Steve Ballmer, the CEO of Microsoft; Jeff Bewkes, the CEO of Time Warner; Peter Thiel, founder of PayPal; and Jerry Yang and David Filo, founders of Yahoo! To name a few...

Stanford wants the crazy-brilliant students who have passions so intense and so focused that they can ignore the distractions of the many activities that the well-rounded students spend their time doing.

Stanford's approach aligns with current research. The quickest way to wrap your mind around this area of study is to read the book *Outliers: The Story of Success* by Malcolm Gladwell (2009). Gladwell's book is based in many different scientific approaches to figuring out why some people succeed and some people do not.

I absorbed the concept of outliers by listening to the audiobook. Whenever my husband and I were driving somewhere, I turned on the audiobook in the car. It is the best way for my husband with AS to read the book. He has not read a whole book in years due to certain sensory issues, but listening while driving—that is the key for him.

Everyone's different. That is OK. Well-rounded is not the goal.

This particular Best Practice sprang from a friendship with the woman to whom I partly dedicated this book. Rebekah has the wonderfully comforting view that anomalies are meant to be embraced. We all have diagnosable parts of our selves. Be beautiful anyway: "Let your freak flag fly!"

It should be noted that Rebekah has achieved success in several fields, as a comedian, an artist, and now as a mother. When you look at her face (if you can see her face) there is beauty, vibrancy, and a depth that most people simply do not develop. Rebekah is painfully alive and, by all standard measures, successful. She is also not aiming for balance.

There are many, many jobs where an imbalance is *required.* Personally, I do not know of any successful artists who are both successful and well-rounded. Note that, for an artist, success is usually defined by society accepting and appreciating their work by valuing it highly.

Artists actually need (what is perceived by most as) an imbalance. They need an overpowering obsession that allows them to immerse themselves completely in their work so intensely that they forget all other distractions. In the immersion they develop mastery.

Another example is a position in the legal field. Attorneys, judges, and many of the other staff that work on cases that affect the way our world works need to dive unusually deep into their chosen field. Without this focus, holding a massive amount of data in their brains all at once, they have a lesser shot at winning a case. The legal field also often requires that the lawyer have little or no caring for the people he is against.

This line in the diagnosis states that the impairment must be in a significant area of functioning. Here are the top three that, from my view as an employer, could be seen as either impairments or assets depending on which side of the coin you wish to view:

1. self-help skills

2. executive function

3. social functioning.

The second and third were discussed previously, but the first, self-help skills, has not been discussed yet.

Self-help skills, include dressing yourself, personal hygiene, feeding yourself adequately, and generally taking care of yourself in ways that your parents probably did for you when you were younger.

I love the flip side of this coin.

Let's start with the funniest example.

In offices that employ many programmers it is actually a *disadvantage* to dress nicely.

As Joy, a project manager for a software company, says, "Wear a suit to a job interview for a programming position and there is no way I will hire you. It shows that you have never had a real job as a programmer before."

In the tech sector, led by people similar to Bill Gates, in the US at least, offices were staffed by people who were more interested in creating great software than they were in dressing nicely for the job. They were working 16 hours, 18 hours a day during a deadline, sleeping at the office. Who had time for hygiene when the project was behind schedule?

Here is my favorite part: Perhaps this is common, perhaps it is not, but in many of the offices I have known of in the Silicon Valley area, Redmond, Austin, and other tech centers in the US, there is a bit of competitiveness regarding who is working hardest for a deadline.

This competitiveness for working the hardest is shown by how little time you spend on personal hygiene. When you are working hard, you do not have time for changing your clothes, shaving, or showering.

We have seen many men—my husband included—actually grow beards during particularly long deadlines simply because they did not have time to shave.

During one particularly long deadline, more than a year, my husband's hair grew so long that he began using a ponytail holder to keep it out of his eyes.

When the deadline finished and he finally came out of the haze of the deadline, he noticed how long his hair was. I cut it for him at home so that:

1. he could avoid the stress of going to a hairdresser, and

2. so the kids could watch their Daddy get his hair cut. I was worried that the children would not recognize Michael as he morphed from the alpha male of the previous deadline to a clean-cut, clean-shaven professional man.

Let it be noted that his hair length was the longest on the team and, yes, he was given the biggest bonus upon project completion.

It is worth asking: Does hygiene even matter? This is one question you should ask yourself before you go to the effort to do all the many things that you might prefer not to do every day.

Does it really matter that you wear an ironed shirt to work? Does it really matter that your hair is professionally cut every six weeks? Does it really matter that you are wearing the latest style?

If the answers to those questions are a full "yes" in your workplace then please do make the effort to do whatever it takes to care for yourself adequately for your particular line of work.

If you like dressing nicely, even though this is more work for you than it may be for others, then go ahead and do it. The goal is for you to be comfortable on the job and successful based on what is generally acceptable in your particular work environment.

Here are a few general rules used by successful Aspies worldwide:

1. Wear only plain colors: no stripes, plaids, or checkered shirts.

2. Choose colors that you have seen worn together in magazine ads. For example, in the window of a clothing store, my husband saw a mannequin with a black t-shirt and dark jeans. He went in and bought a black t-shirt and dark jeans. It is one of his preferred outfits.

3. Once you find a shirt that fits you well, buy five of them, but not all in the same color. If you wear the same color, same style shirt every day, *even if it is not the same shirt as the day before*, people will think you have not changed your clothes. In some parts of the world, this is fine, but in most of the tech centers I have visited, it would be in your best interest to wear new clothes each day.

4. Once you find pants that fit, buy five pairs. People are far more tolerant of the same pants being worn again and again. For example, Bill Gates has worn tan pants most of his adult life. He may wear the same pair a few days in a row—I would not know—but people generally overlook if the pants look the same as the day before.

5. Why go to the effort of making sure you look nice? Because it is easier to get what you want when you dress nicely. In my own experience, I have found that *every time* I have worn a white button-down shirt when taking an airplane flight I get much better service. My seat is upgraded; sometimes I even get an earlier flight; people go out of their way to help me; and more than once a flight has been held for me and me alone...because the nice shirt and pretty skirt made people believe I was "worth it." Whether these value judgements are accurate or not, the underlying message is undeniable—people judge based on appearance.

"___ (name of colleague), I've been working here for ___ (length of time) and I'm just not sure what is the appropriate dress code. What's the general dress code here?"

Then, after paying close attention to the answer, you can ask follow-up questions appropriate to your culture/country. For the US, the questions may be:

"Is there a different dress code on Fridays?"

"What do people usually wear to important meetings/the company meetings?"

"When people come in for overtime on the weekends, do they still dress like they do during the week?"

Only ask this last question if people normally dress nicely at work. If the dress code is t-shirt and jeans, then the only more casual attire is pajamas. It is probably never OK to wear your pajamas to work.

Who You Are at Work

While I would love to say "This part of the diagnostic criteria indicates that there was no clinically significant general delay in language and therefore the person with AS is able to communicate efficiently on the job," such a statement would be erroneous.

You may experience significant communication difficulties that become unfortunately noticeable on the job. These difficulties are based in the tangle of social messages, body language, and gestures that are often part of regular employment.

Best Practice 38: The Thoughtful Pause, a Sign of Wisdom

Light travels faster than sound. This is why some people appear bright until you hear them speak.

—Common saying

One of the most brilliant tactics to ease the strain of social relations is the tactic of "appearing brilliant."

When someone asks you a question, do not answer immediately unless it is an easy to answer question. Wait a few seconds before replying.

Whether you pause in a communication to give something thought or just to give yourself space, a thoughtful pause can gain you several advantages.

First advantage: Talking less gives a perception of intelligence.

I have heard people say, "I thought he was smart until he opened his mouth." This is not a new concept, but rather a centuries-old one:

> *Even a fool is thought wise if he keeps silent, and discerning if he holds his tongue.*
>
> —The Bible, Proverbs 17:28

Second advantage: It does actually give you time to consider a reasonable response. With that extra two or three seconds you can consider many things.

Third advantage: Many people ask questions just to hear themselves talk, not because they want an actual response from you. Sometimes, when you pause, the person talking will fill in the answer themselves, thus alleviating you of the responsibility of replying at all.

It is a far greater risk, especially in a work environment, to talk excessively when social communication is something that does not come naturally. In this area, you can use your AS-based "impairment" to channel your energy towards a highly beneficial communication strategy at work.

If you have a hard time remembering the thoughtful pause, the following image and rhyme may help:

> *A wise old owl sat in an oak.*
> *The more he saw, the less he spoke.*
> *The less he spoke, the more he heard.*
> *Why can't we be like that wise old bird?*
>
> —Old English Nursery Rhyme

It also pays to remember that, if you can master the act of listening carefully and communicating thoughtfully, your verbal interactions will not only be successful more often, but others will wish they were like you, like "a wise old owl…"

Best Practice 39: Shift Expectations
Internally and at Work

Expectations shape who we become.

If a child has "no significant delay," he will be treated as a "normal" child growing up. How adults treat a child when young deeply affects the type of person that child becomes. Certain skills are highlighted and embraced while certain actions will be punished or ignored. One simple example: A studious child growing up in a home where athletic ability is most valued will have a much smaller chance of having her academic achievements recognized.

In the context of the AS diagnosis, if a child appears normal—if she can get her clothes on properly (self-help skills), do her math and reading just fine (cognitive development), and is sufficiently curious about the world, as other children are—then the child will also be expected to have good eye-to-eye gaze, good communication abilities, and so on.

Compare this to how a child with an obvious disability is viewed and treated. Whether it is a genetic anomaly apparent in the child's physiology or a type of physical assistance he or she needs such as a wheelchair, when that child is seen as "disabled" the adults *expect* there to be other "problems." When they care for the child they are far more receptive to and tolerant of mistakes that child might make. There is a clear and obvious explanation.

What happens when a child with AS appears normal and is treated as "normal"? Many inaccurate assumptions can be made and these assumptions shape the child in many ways. How you are shaped as a child in part determines the struggles you will face as an employed adult.

My original training is as a school teacher. In the US the type of training I received covered certification from kindergarten (5 years old) to 12th grade (18 years old). I loved teaching, especially the younger ages, and my stack of books for leisure reading were all non-fiction child development books. Within those books I found study after study proving that *expectations change performance*.

seem to shift in each environment, when in truth it is simply a coping mechanism of someone trying to do what is best.

This ability to shift one's persona is a skill and should not be seen as yet another disability. To keep this AS trait strong and vital while maintaining your sense of self, it may be helpful to solidify your core sense of self.

How? Collect a set of good photos of yourself. Make sure these photos showcase the best aspects of who you are. Michael's photos over the years have been:

- Riding bikes with his children near a beautiful lake.

- With me in Hong Kong.

- His kids hugging him.

- With me in Paris.

- At his own desk at work.

- Relaxing while driving a nice car.

These photos represent the aspects of himself that he wants to be most prominent in his mind. These images of himself are positive, good, and strong.

If you cannot pull together the photos yourself, ask a friend or family member to help you. Post the photos in a place you see naturally every day both at home or at work. Note of caution: If you do have pictures of yourself at work, have only one or two that are of yourself. Taping ten pictures of yourself to your cubicle wall may make you look self-centered. Taping one or two pictures of yourself and another one or two pictures of you with your cat, with your friend, or with anyone else can give people a positive impression of you since they also see your pictures occasionally.

Do this whether you have a positive self-image, a negative image, or not much of an image at all. Do this whether you are currently successful at work or only aiming to be successful someday.

Why? Because the good parts of ourselves should be the biggest parts of ourselves.

Consider the alternative—would you rather focus on the difficulties, the struggles, the heartache, the burning pain of social rejection, the humiliation of "not getting it," the agony of not being able to figure out what someone wants you to do?

Focus on the positives and the negatives disappear.

Best Practice 41: When
"Othering" Happens at Work

One final warning Best Practice before launching into the final one and the close of the book: There is a nasty thing people do when they want to pretend that they are better than someone else. They talk about you as if you are an "other."

In psychology this concept is explained as the "I/Thou" versus "I/It" concept. When you see another person as a human being such as yourself, someone worthy of respect and love, you see them as a "Thou." When you devalue the other person, stripping them of the identifying traits that make them human, you have objectified them and they are now an "It."

You may have a hard time identifying what is actually occurring when a colleague is speaking to you as an "It." The intangibles in social situations can sometimes be hard to identify. So, I will use an extreme example to show:

1. how othering occurs

2. how the dehumanizing is only a matter of viewpoint, not reality, and

3. how to recover from it.

Here is the example: Several years ago, during a three-week Christmas holiday from school, I took my two oldest sons to Israel. The purpose was to help them better understand the Israeli-Palestinian conflict that was being discussed in their high school classes. We also wanted to see the land where so many historical events had taken place.

On our last day in Jerusalem, we had the free time to walk to the Holocaust museum. It was not at all what I expected. It was artistically built, but the way the information was presented was clinical, historical, without the typical visual images of mass death (although these images were in the later part of the museum). For the first two hours we were in the museum, we saw and learned about how the Jewish people had been dehumanized in the press.

How do you dehumanize an entire population to such a level? The main reason that the German guards, soldiers, and various leaders were able to kill people who, truth be told, looked not-so-different from themselves is because the Jewish people had been completely dehumanized. *They were no longer human.* At least, that was the perception that allowed the atrocities to occur.

First, the media began drawing caricatures in the newspapers showing well-known Jewish leaders with massively large noses, and other grotesque non-human features. The illustrations and articles became progressively worse until neighbor turned against neighbor.

Were Jewish people any less human than their captors? No. Were they any less valuable? No. It was a matter of perception and power.

This is an extreme example and should be used only to see the most extreme outcome of a massively large portion of the world engaging in othering to a horrifying degree.

Everyone is capable of, and often engages in, smaller acts of othering. Othering is a simple dynamic that occurs on a smaller scale all over the world probably every day. It even happens in the workplace. It starts with mocking the person openly and ends with the person being seen as less than human. While it is good to ignore most situations where you are left out, forgotten, or otherwise cut off from the group, if it becomes severe then it may help to recognize it for what it is and work to fix the problem.

It is important to turn this dynamic around and make sure that the people that you work with treat you with respect and general human kindness. While most people, AS or not, are treated as "Its" often, it is important to be careful that this does not become the norm in your work environment.

With AS, especially if you have full mindblindness, you are at particularly high risk of othering your co-workers. Since the person with mindblindness does not recognize that people have minds at all, they are automatically and naturally other. If you treat someone like an It, they are highly likely to treat you like an It in return.

If you are seeing othering occur in your work environment, first look to see if you caused it in the first place and fix that problem. After stabilizing how you see them (even if it is not natural for you to think of others as independent, intelligent people just like yourself) then you can work on getting respect in return.

If you have verified that you are not the one causing the othering, how do you go about solving the othering that is coming from co-workers? It may help to talk to someone about whether or not your perception of the problem is correct. Prepare to be wrong. Be relieved and glad if it is simply a misunderstanding.

Before you talk to the boss, colleague, human resources staff, or whomever you believe would be most likely to help you figure out what to do next, sit down and write a list of perceived slights. It is always important that any significant difficulty at work be well-documented.

Note that problems such as "The guys never ask me to go to lunch with them" or "The boss seems to like ___ better" are not worth your energy or time. Some people like other people better. It is not something you necessarily need to fix unless you really want the boss to like you or you really want to go out to lunch with the guys.

The situation that does warrant action is when co-workers are othering you based on your particular autistic traits. The way to tell the difference between what is important and what is not is by asking yourself the question, "Do I need this in order to perform my job well?" If the answer is no, do not let the issue cause you any more stress or time. If the answer is yes, pursue a solution.

When you approach the person who could possibly help you solve the othering problem, ask the following:

"I have been noticing something and I'd like to know your opinion on it. I'm hoping I'm wrong, but it seems like I'm being excluded from ___ and I need to be part of it in order to perform my job properly. Do you have any ideas how I can fix this?"

Other variations may include:

"…it seems like I am not one of the valued team members, yet I am contributing as much as the others… I need to be considered part of the team in order to perform my job properly. Do you have any ideas how I can fix this?"

or

"…it feels like the team sees me as an outsider… I need to be in on the important discussions so I can help contribute to the project too. Do you have any ideas how I can accomplish this?"

Listen carefully. If an answer is given, great. If an answer is not given, take note and try again later or perhaps ask a different colleague. In most companies, the human resources department will help you if no one else can.

Note that nearly everyone feels like an "other" at work, at home, and in society at some point. Othering should not be confused with loneliness, something we all feel throughout a significant portion of our lives. Feeling left out is not a worrisome situation—it is part of what we all experience at work, at home, and at all places we travel.

Loneliness…is and always has been the central and inevitable experience of every man.

—Thomas Wolfe

Loneliness is normal. Othering is more common than it should be. Let most othering slide by without worrying about it. But when othering makes it hard to complete your job, then figure out how to stop its effects.

Best Practice 42: Asserting Your Opinion Confidently Without Being Labeled Narcissistic or Otherwise Unpleasant

He who is unable to live in society, or who has no need because he is sufficient for himself, must be either a beast or a God.

—*Aristotle*

The AS diagnostic criteria does not mention narcissism in particular, but in the work setting it is far too easy for colleagues to label you a narcissist. This is a damaging, hurtful label when it is so inappropriately placed as a description of your motivation and behavior.

AS is easily confused with narcissism due to mindblindness and various issues that give people the wrong impression. In order to understand it more completely, let's look at the narcissism diagnostic criteria according to the *Diagnostic and Statistical Manual of Mental Disprders* the DSM-IV.

Narcissism: In order for a person to be diagnosed with narcissistic personality disorder (NPD) they must meet five or more of the following symptoms:

- being preoccupied with fantasies of unlimited success, power, brilliance, beauty, or ideal love

- believing that he or she is "special" and unique and can only be understood by, or should associate with, other special or high-status people (or institutions)

- requiring excessive admiration

- having a sense of entitlement, i.e., unreasonable expectations of especially favorable treatment or automatic compliance with his or her expectations

- being interpersonally exploitative, i.e., takes advantage of others to achieve his or her own ends

- lacking empathy: being unwilling to recognize or identify with the feelings and needs of others

- being often envious of others or believing that others are envious of him or her

- showing arrogant, haughty behaviors or attitudes.

Mindblindness is a trait where you cannot see that other people have minds different from your own. It is evident when someone tries to communicate a point of view that differs from your own. You will naturally reject it because you see no other valid point of view other than your own.

Let's contrast two men to differentiate between AS and narcissism.

George is opinionated. When others try to assert their opinions in regular day-to-day conversation, George dismisses this as not relevant. George can understand that others have differing points of view—he listens to talk radio and, whenever his favorite host presents a new idea, George aligns his own beliefs with the host's. George believes that most people are stupid because they do not seem to understand "reality."

Reality is whatever George defines as reality since he dismisses all other opinions as wrong. George has been fired many times for dismissing his boss's opinion as irrelevant if it does not match what George already believes to be true. George is capable of grasping other people's viewpoints, but chooses not to because his personal beliefs are that he is right and the rest of the world is wrong.

George is not autistic. He is simply a mean man who makes people miserable. He has many issues that could possibly be solved with a therapist's intervention but George is too busy proving everyone wrong.

In contrast, Joe also sees his opinion as the only valid one, but when he was younger, his father told him very clearly, "Joe, people are trying to help you. Be nice. These are good people." In Joe's view, since he can see no other truth other than his own perception of the world, he sees the choices people make and they appear as stupid choices. But, Joe does not interfere. He knows, thanks to his loving and persistent father, that people are good. Stupid, but good. Joe can respect people in general, although he does pity them a little, especially when they make such obviously illogical choices.

As an adult Joe was diagnosed with Asperger Syndrome. His mindblindness is based in how his neurology is shaped. While this mindblindness could be crippling, it is not. Joe generally keeps quiet when he sees people making stupid mistakes.

Safety, Survival and the Ultimate Success

This final section of the book is the section I hope you turn to on difficult days. I hope you review the content here when you are confused, hurt, or otherwise struggling in your career (and we all struggle at times).

I have put together the three concepts that a person would be most likely to review when in a difficult situation: safety, survival, and your rights. When you are stressed and deep into overload, it is not a good time to think about your career path or how to manage difficult co-worker relationships. During difficult times, it is best to focus on healing and building your tolerance and health with suggestions like those in this section.

The Safety Point

Everyone has a range of performance ability, a scale on which they can either thrive or fail. It is a vertical scale that generally functions as follows:

Thriving, fully engaged, contributing best skills to world
↓

Engaged in work at a semi-successful level, getting by
↓

Completing work, surviving but miserable
↓

Not completing all projects that need to be completed

↓

SAFETY POINT

↓

Struggling to complete basic life tasks

↓

Anger or detachment

↓

Serious depression, suicidal thoughts, extreme burn-out

This vertical scale helps us in many situations describe and quantify the many aspects of Aspie life. One poignant example follows:

Because of Michael's hyper-focus on work, he often works at night after the children and I have gone to bed. His focus is so intense that he often forgets what time it is and does not go to bed until early morning.

Unfortunately, he has obligations in the morning. He wakes up after only a few hours of sleep and is on auto-pilot, just going through the motions, working below the "safety line."

It may help you to put a numerical value on this scale. For example, every hour past midnight that he is up working is a -10 to his ability to function the next day. A big, sugary, caffeine-loaded soda in the morning may help him wake up but it is a -25 to his ability to function later in the day. Enough negatives and he is in a dangerous zone where all comments from others are perceived as negative and everything is an offense. Any request from another person (except the request "Please get some sleep") is considered an aggressive act of control. The only way to get out of the danger zone in this particular example is for him to sleep until he is rested and back above the "safety line."

A good workout is a $+10$, a full night's sleep is a $+25$, eating a healthy breakfast is a $+5$. He is in control of how well he is able to function and there is a clear, visual, quantifiable way to track it. When he is feeling awful, there is a way to look back and count the number of things (or the intensity of one thing) that made life so difficult. It reduces the sense of loss of control.

people are rejuvenated by meetings, a positive, while some people are drained by meetings, a negative. The degree to which this affects you is based on your own internal gauge.

When you recognize and respect your own personal negatives (and positives) you have a straighter path to health. One man with AS, Darren, said, "But keeping myself above the safety line is a luxury I can't afford." Darren has a difficult career in a difficult field—real estate—a job not well-suited to how he works naturally. He needs a predictable day yet clients call at all hours requesting that he change his schedule on the spot. Darren does not enjoy face-to-face interactions, yet nearly all of his work involves face-to-face meetings. His career provides non-stop negatives that keep Darren below the safety line. In Darren's case, recognizing the safety line may provide enough motivation to help him switch careers someday.

In our daily work, it is crucial that we recognize overload and respect the consequences of ignored long-term damage. Overload is real. It can be brutal. It can cause intense physical, psychological, and even spiritual pain. In a work environment you may be required to do things such as give presentations, make phone calls, or interact socially in ways that are so far beyond your comfort level that your deepest, most primal safety mechanisms will kick in. An employee (or boss) in self-protection mode can get little actual work done.

In your *42 Best Practice Notebook* mentioned in Best Practice 23, make a page titled *Survival Toolkit Top 10.*

Survival Toolkit Top 10

On this page (and I hope many following pages) you will be listing the many things you can do to pull yourself high enough above the safety line to live a happy, successful life. A happy, successful person is a good employee or employer. This toolkit should be your launching pad for building your own list of positives.

Below I give you a potential Top 10 of survival techniques to start with. These may be things you are currently doing, or things that you might like to try next time you feel yourself dipping.

These are the standard Top 10 that are most likely to fit any Aspie regardless of specific differences. Just like aspirin works for a wide variety of illnesses, there are some basic techniques that *just work* for nearly anyone.

Once you have finished the Top 10, please, dear reader, go beyond this list. We are not all alike. You will have survival strategies that are unlike any others. Temple Grandin, a well-known woman with AS, developed a survival strategy involving machinery meant for feeding cows (deep body pressure) (Grandin 2006). Numerous other Aspies have given their strategies for success by explaining their own unique solutions. Some of yours may include:

- 10 minutes in a closet. Try it. It can be quite relaxing.

- 15 minutes underneath 15 heavy blankets, or, if at work, 15 minutes with a heavy coat on.

- Heavy metal music listened to on headphones with the volume turned up so loud your ears buzz afterwards. Pick the style that works for you. Heavy metal is the style that works for one particular young woman, Annabella, with AS.

- 10 minutes of pillow fighting, a strategy that worked for my husband and sons.

- An entire Saturday of reading, getting out of bed only to eat and use the restroom. Household chores can wait. If you need to come above the safety line, do whatever it takes to get there.

- An evening of computer gaming. Massively multi-player online games, MMOGs, are often comforting for Aspies (as long as the games do not become addictive).

- Engaging in a particular hobby, perhaps knitting during your lunch hour.

- Clean something. Anything. Create order out of chaos if that is what relaxes you.

- A particular sport, perhaps done before or after work. One Aspie goes skateboarding before work. The falls and "accidents" are, strangely, what help him most. The deep and often painful impact somehow wakes him to us sufficiently. There has been no permanent damage yet and it seems to work for him.

- Find a way to lie upside down so all the blood rushes to your head; spin in circles; do somersaults. Do whatever it takes to get your sensory system back in gear.

Open your mind to the wonderful things, no matter how bizarre, that honestly and truly rejuvenate you.

What if next time you have a difficulty at work, you have a list of 10 things to check that might help you see things more clearly? Just as people with diabetes often have a candy bar in their purse or pocket for emergencies, a person with AS may have the following "tools" on a card in their purse or pocket. If you don't carry them with you, at least have these techniques in the back of your mind in case of overload.

Survival technique 1: Breathe

I hope you have enough Mr. Spock logic in you to see why "Breathe" is listed first. It is the most primal. Primal means "being first in time" (standard medical dictionary definition).

When there is a problem, it helps to look at the most fundamental underlying cause first. Are you breathing well? Is your brain getting sufficient oxygen to work properly?

You would think this would be obvious, correct? Not so! There are innumerable studies that show that brain function slows down when deprived of oxygen and a few more studies showing that we tend to breathe shallowly, insufficiently. Why would a person consciously deprive herself of something so life-giving as oxygen?

Follow this logic:

1. Stress can cause a decreased intake of oxygen.

2. Social situations can cause stress.

3. Various aspects of AS cause a great potential for difficulty in social situations.

For example, one woman with Asperger Syndrome, Stacey, consistently, consciously slows her oxygen intake. It makes clear thought difficult for her. When stressed, usually when in conversation with someone, she "forgets to breathe." This may be more common than most people realize.

Stacey usually catches it and can self-correct, but when the stress is intense, she will actually pass out. Passing out is a body's way of overriding your nervous system's mistake. Here is how it goes: Stacey senses stress; her body goes into self-protective mode and stops breathing in a primitive effort to "hide" from the predator. (It is harder for a predator to identify prey that is completely still.)

While the airflow is cut off, the oxygen to her brain slows and the body reacts to compensate for the sudden loss. Generally, the adrenal glands will respond by flooding the body with adrenaline, stimulating a sense of panic in the person who has slowed or stopped breathing.

In a person with AS, who may be accustomed to a persistent sense of panic in social situations, there may be a less noticeable internal warning sign due to something called adrenal fatigue.

If the adrenaline-filled warning is not heeded, the body takes measures into its own hands and you faint. It is your body's last-ditch effort to get the oxygen flowing again. A business-related analogy would be a large company shutting down a main branch of the store during a recession.

The medical term for fainting is *syncope*. This insufficient oxygen in the brain is known as the medical condition *cerebral hypoxia* (Lempert 1996).

Passing out allows the body's natural flow of oxygen to resume. The oxygen flows back in through your lungs, redistributes evenly, and you wake up once your brain is sufficiently oxygenated.

While this is the most severe reaction, there are many more common symptoms caused by holding your breath. You may have

If you are not yet convinced that breath-work is an important practice for you, perhaps this last reason will convince you that it is worth the effort.

Survival technique 2: Drink water

What could be more obvious than staying hydrated? It may be obvious, but it is so easily overlooked. Although no markedly reputable statistics exist for determining the percentage of people who are dehydrated at any given time, some estimates are as high as "75 percent of Americans are chronically dehydrated" (Peter Ragnar, "You're Not Demented, Just Dehydrated" 2009).

A mere 2 percent drop in a body's hydration can cause mental fuzziness. It slows brain function. Sensory overload is more likely to occur. Brainspace shrinks. Abilities shut down. It simply is not worth the cost.

The average person needs eight glasses of water per day. Consider your own personal schedule and set a regular plan for achieving proper hydration. For someone who is generally routine-driven, this task may be easier for you than for others without AS.

Take a minute to write out your regular daily schedule. Add in the times when you would refill your water cup, bottle, jug, or other water container. Here is what my day looks like:

- 6am: Wake up—*Glass 1*
- 7am: Kids up—*Glass 2*
- 8am: Kids to school
- 9am: Begin work—*Glass 3*
- 10am: Meeting
- 11am: Regular work—*Glass 4*
- 12 noon: Lunch
- 1pm: Work
- 2pm: Work—*Glass 5*

- 3pm: 30 minute break/work
- 4pm: Work—*Glass 6*
- 5pm: Pick up kids/workout—*Glass 7*
- 6pm: Dinner
- 7pm: Clean house
- 8pm: Children to bed—*Glass 8*
- 9pm: Work
- 10pm: Bed

Of course there is variety day-to-day. There are additional meetings, night-time obligations, and trips, but having a regular schedule helps me see when I should get that cup of water. It is a vital baseline.

As you draft your own routine, there are several general rules to follow:

- Front-load your water intake. Drinking two glasses right before bed makes it more likely that you will wake up in the night to use the restroom, disrupting your sleep.

- Drink water before a meal, not during a meal. This helps you eat less during the meal.

- Take sips of water during a workout. During a spinning workout (cycling) the instructor prompts us to take a sip of water every four to five minutes. It makes the workout quite pleasant. During an intense aerobic workout it is important to drink slowly as the body has a hard time absorbing large quantities of water at once.

- Schedule your water intake during times when it will be easy to remember to drink. When you first sit down at your desk in the morning, make sure you have a fresh cup of water at your desk.

Note that coffee, caffeinated tea, and energy drinks have a diuretic effect. They dehydrate your body. The effect may be obvious if you pay attention. Try going without coffee for a week, then have a coffee one morning along with your regular water intact. You will probably find yourself using the restroom an unpleasant number of times as your body strips itself of its available water supply.

While it is important to stay hydrated, keep in mind that there is a condition called *hyper-hydration*, water poisoning or water intoxication, when the body is processing such a large quantity of fluid that the normal balance of electrolytes is pushed outside of safe limits. It can be serious enough to cause death. This usually only happens during drinking contests or long drawn-out exercise such as marathons where water is consumed, but not enough electrolytes.

It has been widely documented that proper water intake improves mental function. When you are working with a brain highly susceptible to overload and you are in an environment that causes overload, you can take this simple, easy measure to improve your chances of success.

Survival technique 3: Exercise

I wish there was a book titled *Exercise and the Autistic Brain* written by an occupational therapist or an MD. For the purposes of this book, I did enough research to give the basics. It would be wonderful to see the details and specifics outlined by a well-trained professional.

Why is regular exercise linked to professional success for someone with Asperger Syndrome?

1. Regular exercise calms the nervous system.

2. Both aerobic (jogging, cycling, dance) and anaerobic exercise (yoga, walking) increase blood flow. Blood flow to the brain increases the brain's ability to function effectively. This helps in every area of your work performance.

3. Exercise, especially coupled with a healthy diet, builds a healthy, attractive body. In every culture, every environment, people are attracted to and generally give greater respect to beautiful people.

This is an unpleasant and unfortunate fact—it would be a nicer world if we were judged by the content of our character instead of the shape of our bodies. But, this is one area where you can make a small difference for yourself personally. It is well-documented that fit people earn more money. It does not mean that fit people are more happy or are better people, just that careers tend to be easier to build when your body is in good shape.

> *Those who think they have not time for bodily exercise will sooner or later have to find time for illness.*
>
> *—Edward Stanley*

Survival technique 4: Eat well

There are many health conditions that, according to current research, appear to be co-morbid with autism and AS. There is a chance that you have an underlying allergy, sensitivity, or dietary need that is currently unrecognized. Fixing it may give you a tremendously helpful boost on the job.

Stan was a systems administrator at a research lab. He was often tired, but he figured it was due to the long hours. Stan's mother had often said that he seemed "fuzzy brained" when growing up. Stan's teachers had often chastised him for forgetting to turn in assignments. Stan's colleagues were often angry with him for "not paying attention."

One day Stan's mother called him and said, "Stan, I just found out I am gluten intolerant. Can you try avoiding gluten for a while?" Stan's mother knew he was too fuzzy brained to follow-through on such a vague request so she gave him a quick and easy summation of what he needed to do: "If it's not a vegetable, fruit, meat, or dairy don't eat it."

The next morning, Stan looked at the big blueberry muffin he was going to eat. It was mostly a big, white fluffy cake with little blueberries dotting it. Instead of eating the muffin, he got two eggs out of the refrigerator and fried them. He put a piece of cheese on top and had breakfast. During lunch, he skipped the pizza because of the pizza crust and instead had tacos with corn tortillas. For dinner, he stopped by the local farmer's market and purchased a bag full of vegetables he recognized.

At home, he cut up several of them, put them in a bowl, poured ranch dressing on them, and ate them while working on his computer. That evening Stan felt better than he ever had. He usually went to bed tired, but this evening he was able to read a science fiction book for an hour before falling asleep. He had purchased that particular science fiction book years ago but had always been too tired at night to even pick it up.

The next morning Stan woke up well-rested, a feeling he had only felt rarely. As Stan stuck to the "fruit, vegetable, meat, or dairy" rule, his mental fog cleared. By the end of the fourth day, the difference was significant enough to cause his colleagues to comment.

Most people with gluten intolerance take weeks, months, and sometimes years to clean the body, but for some, the change is almost immediate.

Note that, if you are gluten intolerant and follow a gluten-free diet for long enough to change your body chemistry, your body drops its defenses to the gluten.

If you happen to make a mistake and consume gluten, you may suffer a severe reaction. Personally, I am gluten-intolerant and I was able to see improvement within the first week. After the first month, I felt better than I ever had.

But one day I had a difficult meeting in a town that was more than an hour's drive from my office. I had recently purchased snacks for the staff break room, including a big bucket of red licorice. I grabbed a whole handful and told myself that I would have them as a reward on my drive home if the meeting went well. It was highly motivating for me because I loved red licorice as a kid.

On the way home I began happily munching the licorice. It tasted wonderful, but I noticed that I was getting sleepy, close to being too sleepy to drive. By the time I was near home I was considering calling it a sick day.

I went in to work anyway and explained to an assistant that I was not feeling well. She had seen me grab a handful of licorice and asked if that could be the problem. I told her that, no, that is ridiculous. Licorice does not have wheat in it.

A few hours later, I felt like I was getting the flu. My throat was sore, my legs were weak. I was dizzy and so sleepy I could barely keep my eyes open. I found myself in the kitchen, getting a drink and looking for something with caffeine that would help me stay awake long enough to finish the work day.

The jar of licorice was sitting on the counter, so in my haze, I read the ingredients list. Wheat was the number one ingredient!

It took three days to regain my strength. There have been other mistakes since then, but in general I try to be as careful as possible to avoid this toxin in my body.

Pay attention to how your body responds to the food you intake. It affects your work performance.

Life is not merely being alive, but being well.—Martial

Survival technique 5: Sleep

Sleep is the ultimate healer. For people with AS in particular, sleep can:

- calm the sensory system

- rejuvenate the mind's ability to deal with interruption

- increase flexibility, and much more.

Even if it means taking an afternoon nap during your lunch hour, ensuring adequate sleep is a vital survival tool. One man with AS who works at a company designing medical devices uses his lunch hour for a nap. He sits in his car in the parking lot, tilts the seat back, and takes a nap. He sets his watch alarm to wake him up after 25 minutes and he returns to the office rejuvenated. On the days when he misses this nap, he experiences enough overload that he often has to go home early.

What if sleep is difficult for you? What if you wake in the night or otherwise do not get the sleep you need? Try the following:

- Chamomile tea.

- A dinner geared towards inducing sleep: potatoes, milk, and other foods with sedative qualities.

- Sleeping medicine such as chewable melatonin or prescription medication.

- Meditation CDs. These have been highly effective for every person I have recommended them to and followed up with. Meditation is particularly useful for people who "think in pictures" (a term coined by Temple Grandin). Many meditations involve the visualization of an environment that can be quite pleasant for someone who enjoys the creative act of visualization.

- Clearing your bedroom of all distractions.

- A routine to sleep. For example: Lie down. Straighten body. Adjust pillow. Straighten body again. Breathe deeply 20 times.

Sleep deprivation sounds innocuous enough. Missing a few extra hours every night cannot hurt physically; it just makes you tired the next day, right? Not so. Sleep deprivation is just as harmful as food deprivation or water deprivation. They can all cause severe health problems.

A few more side effects of sleep deprivation:

- aching muscles

- dizziness and nausea

- dry mouth

- hallucinations

- hand tremors

- headaches

- increased blood pressure

- increased risk of diabetes

- increased risk of fibromyalgia

- irritability

- memory lapses or loss

- nystagmus (rapid involuntary rhythmic eye movement)

- obesity

- slowed word recall

- temper tantrums in children

- yawning

- symptoms similar to:

  o attention-deficit hyperactivity disorder (ADHD)

  o psychosis.

A well-rested employee is a good employee. More than once I have sent an employee home to rest, especially employees who are paid hourly. When you are sleep deprived, not only is it difficult to complete work, it is difficult to produce quality work. The error rate increases drastically based on the level of sleep deprivation.

One great way to keep your job and improve your career is to sleep well. If you need help achieving a better night's sleep, contact a physician who can work with your particular physical responses to sleep.

Survival technique 6: Make a nest

Everyone needs a place to hide, a place to let loose, and relax. This is particularly important when your neurological structure necessitates extra care.

Ideally, you will find a job with an office. And a door. And blinds so that no one can see inside. Ideally, you will be able to close and lock the door, turn the lights off, and lean back in your comfortable chair when needed. A short nap or just a few minutes' rest can be very effective in helping you maintain optimal function on the job.

During a span of eight years of my husband's career, he had just such an office. It made a big difference in the quality of his work.

As he moved from one job to the next, he experienced several different environments. One was where he was in a large theater-sized room with 50 other employees and no walls between desks. The acoustics created massive, constant auditory overload.

In another work environment, he shared a desk with another colleague. His territory was not well-defined so he shrunk his own space until he had very little room to work.

In another, his desk was facing out a large 22 story tall wall of windows. Through these windows came the heat of the afternoon sun and the glare in his eyes was blinding. He never did ask to move to a different desk. Day after day he suffered migraines and sickening ophthalmic pain. His eyesight was probably permanently damaged.

Most people work in environments where the noise, social contact, and visual field are far from optimal. Explore and modify your environment as much as possible to reduce the many strains on your sensory system.

If you can make your office space a nurturing, healthy place, fantastic. If you cannot, then focus your efforts on making your home the place you can use for relaxation and letdown after long, hard days.

One man with AS did this by putting color light bulbs in his lamps at home. When he is in a red mood, he turns on the lamp with the red light. The light is dimmer than a white or clear bulb would give. When he is in a blue mood, he turns on the lamp with a blue bulb. He also has purple bulb and yellow bulb lamps. For $2.95 per bulb, he has managed to create a visual impact at home that he finds soothing.

One woman with AS purchased dozens of pillows and an extra deep couch. At night she piles the pillows in just the right way around her body and on her body, rearranging and rearranging for 15–20 minutes, then she watches TV until bedtime.

One last example of making home a good nest: One man with AS living in Texas found that most homes and apartments were large and spacious. Many had vaulted ceilings, skylights, and plenty of windows. He found this disconcerting, but endured it until he got a job offer on the west coast. He found that he could only afford a tiny apartment.

He found the apartment to be particularly relaxing. A year later, when he was ready to buy a home, he had full knowledge that he liked low ceilings, tight hallways, and small rooms. It made him feel safe to be in a more snug space. When describing his ideal home to the realtor, there were many miscommunications, but he finally figured out that the term to use was "bungalow." He started looking only at bungalows for sale. A bungalow simply means "little house."

He finally found the perfect little house. It had been on the market for months since it had extra skinny walkways and small rooms. Most people thought the layout of the house was inconvenient and a poor use of space, but this one man with AS thought it was ideal. He bought it for a great price and now finds his evenings give him the relaxation he needs to prepare himself for the next day of work.

Find what works for you whether it is visual, auditory (great music in the background), olfactory (candles that smell sweet and delicious), or tactile (hardwood floors or extra thick shag carpet). Find out what your senses crave most, then build a nest that suits you best.

Survival technique 7: Read

Reading may be your ultimate survival strategy. For one Aspie teenager, Ron, reading was the way he learned all of his social skills. Over the years Ron had wanted to know why he could so rarely talk with people well. Ron's parents were not helpful. His teachers were not helpful. So, when Ron entered college as a young adult, he had no social skills training and still plenty of desire to learn.

Ron found college to be easy so he had plenty of time to read. The more fiction books he read, the more he was able to understand the social relationships around him. In fact, he was obsessed with social relationships, making friends simply for the fun of seeing the path the relationship would take.

Often Ron made mistakes. Sometimes he would quote direct passages, but not always from the same book, so that in one conversation he could use grammar from the 1800s as well as grammar from a futuristic science fiction book. But Ron learned quickly and was soon able to craft sentences that created a coherent basis of conversation for most situations.

Near the end of Ron's third year of college, as he was leaving the library one day, he walked through a row of books he normally did not walk through. He saw the 150s section, the psychology books sorted according to the Dewey Decimal system. Ron found so many books he wanted to read that he could not carry them all. He sat in a pile of books for the rest of the day devouring what he could. Ron ended up becoming a successful sociology professor.

Reading can not only be a calming, relaxing activity, but as a survival strategy it is crucial—reading can provide you with insights that you could not get any other way.

When learning job skills, you can learn them either through a person, such as during training, or through an inanimate source, such as a book. Going straight to the book saves you significant time and energy.

Survival technique 8: Indulge in your hobby

Unless your hobby is harmful, too expensive, or otherwise detracts too greatly from your well-being, find a way to engage in it—one hopes as part of your career, but if not, as your free time activity.

Increased means and increased leisure are the two civilizers of man.

— *Benjamin Disraeli*

You will know you have picked the right hobby when you find yourself relaxed and rejuvenated by it.

If you find that you are not relaxed by it, but instead the hobby leaves you a little stressed and less functional, know the hobby is actually an addiction.

The difference between a hobby and an addiction is that a hobby is good for you and an addiction is not.

Addiction is defined by Wikipedia as when "the individual engages in some specific activity, despite harmful consequences, as deemed by the user himself to his individual health, mental state, or social life."

In contrast, during a hobby, the individual engages in some specific activity which creates a sense of comfort, pleasure, and relaxation. Taking time for a hobby will make you a more relaxed, more productive employee.

Survival technique 9: Financial security

We would all love to have "enough" money to be financially secure. But, money does not work that way. A person making the smallest amount of money can often structure his or her life to have that wonderful sense of financial security while a millionaire, especially one who has come by the money suddenly, does not necessarily have that security.

Security is the opposite of risk. Risk is defined as something that involves unknown outcomes. So, security must be a full, or at least as-complete-as-it-can-be, knowledge of the situation.

Financial security as I am referring to it for this purpose is an *awareness* of your financial situation. Once you are aware of your financial situation, you can do what needs to be done to bring your expenses in line with your income.

There is a tremendous difference between those who are financially secure and those who are not. Those who are secure— who know how much money is in the bank now and how much will still be there at the end of the month—are the ones with the greater level of internal relaxation and calm.

Money is at the most foundational, primal level of our need. We need it for food, shelter, and clothing. Knowing that you will have enough to get by will provide you with a sense of satisfaction that you simply cannot get elsewhere.

Having an AS brain positions you far better for financial security than most. You probably already have:

- the ability to review numbers meticulously

- the desire for order and logic

- an aptitude for sufficient focus on the bottomline.

If you are not currently tracking your finances enough to give you that needed sense of financial security, then begin now. Several useful tools are:

- www.mint.com

- www.rudder.com

- www.justthrive.com

Or, if you want a very clear, tight control of finances (that are not too complicated), get a paper register and keep records by hand. There are few things more concrete, more able, to create that sense of financial security, than a paper and pencil money management system.

Whatever you do, look at your personal finances closely enough to eliminate the unknowns, eliminate the risk. This financial security will help boost your confidence, thus making many interactions easier.

Survival technique 10: Check in with friends

Solitude vivifies; isolation kills.—Joseph Roux

This may be your least favorite of the survival tools, but it may be the most important also. Even if you do not like making or keeping friendships, it is important that at least a few people on earth know you are alive.

One example: My husband Michael used to play online games extensively, *Everquest*, *City of Heroes*, and many others. He found a group of friends who have been a tremendous support to him over the years. While they are all virtual, they are as close as friends can be—and much easier to deal with than face-to-face friends.

The group experienced exactly how important their friendships were when one member of the guild (group) went suddenly quiet. The guild member, Jonathan, was on a trip and was playing from his hotel room when he went silent and his online character was obviously "silent." The team members waited the typical amount of time a person needs to reset their Internet connection but still no response from Jonathan.

They recognized the silence as being a red flag. Jonathan had several health issues and, due to the closeness of their friendship, the team members knew that, if he went silent without saying "be right back" or "going to get some food" (but in typical online shorthand), there was probably something wrong.

Several of the team members tracked down the hotel Jonathan was at and called the front desk, asking them to check on him. He was found on the floor, passed out, going into a diabetic coma. While his group of friends were only virtual, they were still friends who were able to do what friends do—help in time of need.

Make and keep a few friendships, not only for safety reasons, but for the more mundane ones also. You may need someone to feed your cats if you have to leave town for some reason. If you get sick there is someone you can call, even if it is a simple email and a few suggestions on how to get better soon.

Friendships are difficult to form as adults, so it may not be the easiest task. Here are a few ways to make friendship-forming a bit easier. Try joining:

- a social group related to your hobby

- a mailing list that you enjoy, or many mailing lists

- a church

- a gym—the YMCA has gyms throughout the work and the Y tends to be particularly Aspie-friendly

- college classes, continuing education either online or at a local university, college, or other type of school

- online game groups that form guilds, corporations, and clans, and other forms of friendship groups

- clubs focused on one interest that you happen to share, such as a club for people interested in ham radio, flight simulators, or chess club.

Participating in social interaction may be less appealing to you than other, more solitary tasks, but the long-term benefit of having a few social connections is worth the effort.

Aspie Bill of Rights—General

In 2006 I started developing co-dependent habits. It was not until 2008 that I noticed them. I had all the classic symptoms: I was other-centered, weak, vulnerable, easily overwhelmed, and I had depressed energy and persistent feelings of guilt.

I worked for several months in 2008 to pull out of the co-dependency, but I kept slipping back into it. One day while browsing the shelves of the local bookstore, I came across a new publication, *The Flight from Intimacy: Healing Your Relationship of Counter-Dependency—The Other Side of Co-Dependency* by Janae B. Weinhold and Barry K. Weinhold (2008).

The insights in *The Flight from Intimacy* saved me and Michael years of difficulty. I worked hard at stopping my most negative co-dependent habits and he also stopped his counter-dependent habits. With both of us working to fix the problem we came out of it relatively fast.

The Flight from Intimacy could have been written for couples with AS. While that was not the author's intent, the counter-dependency they described was as accurate a description of an AS marriage/partnership/close relationship as it could be. With several minor exceptions, the strategies suggested in the book worked. The motivation behind the co-dependent behaviors was often different (usually based in an AS-blindness) but the solutions were the same.

People with AS may appear counter-dependent due to the basics of the diagnostic criteria. Counter-dependency involves avoiding other people, being cut off from your feelings, being self-centered, blaming others, being "armored" against others' attempts to get close, and otherwise avoiding intimacy on any level.

Note that I very carefully said that people with AS *may appear* counter-dependent.

Something as simple as not reflecting an appropriate facial expression at the right time can be interpreted as "being cut off from your feelings." Something as slight as standing too far away from a colleague when he is talking to you can create the impression that you are guarded and have an "armor" against others, that you refuse to engage in meaningful interaction.

The reasons behind the actions are vastly different for a neurotypical and an Aspie, but the solutions suggested were surprisingly helpful.

The section of *The Flight from Intimacy* that provided the biggest mental shift for Michael was the Bill of Rights. It was scary to see how many of these were new thoughts for him.

For example, "10. You have the right to have problems and conflicts. You do not have to be perfect to be loved." Michael expressed that that concept was new to him, something he had never considered before. Within the context of this experience, I drafted an Aspie Bill of Rights pertaining specifically to the AS diagnostic criteria.

Aspie Bill of Rights—General

- You have the right to do whatever it takes to avert meltdown.

- You have the right to self-protect.

- You have the right to feel safe.

- You have the right to set your own rules and boundaries. (There will be consequences but the choice is yours.)

- You have the right to move your body as you wish as long as it does not impinge on the freedoms and safety of others.

- You have the right to use your communicative abilities as you see fit.

- You have the right to choose your friends. While you cannot force someone to be your friend, you can also say no to a friendship if you wish.

- You have the right to experience happiness and fulfilment.

- You have the right to interpret the world as you see it.

- You have a right to privacy and a responsibility to protect the privacy of others.

- You have the right to consider your behaviors as acceptable and normal.

- You have the right to want a good life.

Aspie Bill of Rights—Workplace

Adapted to the work context, the following bill of rights should be of use to you.

Aspie Bill of Rights—Workplace

- You have the right to express your creative talents.

- You have the right to choose your own career.

- You have the right to refuse advancement if the advancement entails unwanted stress. (There may be consequences, but it is your right to not be forced.)

- You have the right to be a manager, a leader, an executive, a boss, a supervisor, or occupy any other "high-level" position if that is something you desire and are willing to train for sufficiently.

- You have the right to choose what you do with your time. (Note that there are consequences to any choice, but the choice is and should be yours.)

- You have the right to pursue professional success. It may not happen in the way you wish, but the pursuit is yours.

- You have the right to immerse yourself in your work.

- You have the right to seek new employment if you wish.

- You have the right to request accommodations.

- You have the right to your own free will.

There are consequences to every one of your actions, but recognizing that they are *your* actions, based in *your* ability to control and manage *your* own life, is an empowering position to be in. The more you fully own your life, the more easily you can direct it.

Summary

To sum up this entire book in two sentences: As a person with an AS neural structure, you have highly valuable unique talents and abilities that can be very beneficial if placed within a healthy environment with caring, understanding colleagues, bosses, and employees. There are many things you can do to facilitate this type of environment.

The 42 Best Practices listed in this book will help you get closer to the happiness that is your basic human right.

It is my deepest personal desire that people with Asperger Syndrome thrive.

References

Allen, D. (2003) *Getting Things Done: The Art of Stress-Free Productivity.* New York and Harmondsworth: Penguin.

Attwood, T. (2008) *The Complete Guide to Asperger's Syndrome.* London and Philadelphia: Jessica Kingsley Publishers.

Ekman, P. and Rosenberg, E.L. (2005) *Facial Action Coding System (FACS) Manual,* 2nd edn. New York: Oxford University Press.

Elder Robison, J. (2009) *Look Me in the Eye: My Life with Asperger's.* London and New York: Ebury Press.

Encyclopedia of Mental Disorders (2010) "Executive Function." www.minddisorders. com/Del-Fi/Executive-function.html.

Gates, B. (1980) Interview with Dennis Bathory-Kitsz, *80 Microcomputing* (magazine).

Gladwell, M. (2009) *Outliers: The Story of Success.* New York and Harmondsworth: Penguin.

Goffee, R. and Jones, G. (2009) *Clever: Leading Your Smartest, Most Creative People.* Boston, MA: Harvard Business School Press.

Goleman, D. (2004) *Destructive Emotions: A Scientific Dialogue with the Dalai Lama.* New York and London: Bantam.

Good, T.L. (1987) "Two decades of research on teacher expectations: Findings and future directions.". *Journal of Teacher Education 38,* 4, 32–47.

Graham, P. (2009) "Maker's Schedule, Manager's Schedule." www.paulgraham.com/ makersschedule.html

Grandin, T. (2006) *Thinking in Pictures: And Other Reports from My Life with Autism.* New York: Knopf Doubleday Publishing Group.

Holliday Willey, L. (1999) *Pretending to Be Normal: Living with Asperger Syndrome.* London and Philadelphia: Jessica Kingsley Publishers.

Jensen, A. (2005) *When Babies Read: A Practical Guide to Helping Young Children with Hyperlexia, Asperger Syndrome and High-Functioning Autism.* London and Philadelphia: Jessica Kingsley Publishers.

Lempert, T. (1996) "Recognizing syncope: Pitfalls and surprises." *Journal of the Royal Society of Medicine 89,* 7, 372–375.

Lencioni, P. (2004) *Death by Meeting: A Leadership Fable…About Solving the Most Painful Problem in Business.* San Francisco, CA: Jossey Bass.

Maslow, A. (1943) "A Theory of Human Motivation." *Psychological Review 50,* 4, 370–396.

Navarro, J. and Karlins, M. (2008) *What Every BODY is Saying: An Ex-FBI Agent's Guide to Speed-Reading People.* New York: Harper Paperbacks.

Peabody, B. (2008) *Lucky or Smart: Fifty Pages for the First-Time Entrepreneur.* Charleston, SC: Booksurge Publishing.

Pease, A. (1981) *Body Language: How to Read Others' Thoughts by Their Gestures (Overcoming Common Problems.)* London: Sheldon Press.

Ragnar, P. (2009) "You're Not Demented, Just Dehydrated." *EnlightenNext Magazine,* September.

Rosenweig, P. (2009) *The Halo Effect...and Eight Other Business Delusions that Deceive Managers.* Reprinted edn. New York: Free Press.

Spolsky, J. (2007) *Smart and Gets Things Done: Joel Spolsky's Concise Guide to Finding the Best Technical Talent.* New York: Apress.

Weinhold, J. and Weinhold, B. (2008) *The Flight from Intimacy: Healing Your Relationship of Counter-Dependency—The Other Side of Co-Dependency.* Novato, CA: New World Library.

Further Reading

Bliss, V. and Edmonds, G. (2007) *A Self-Determined Future with Asperger Syndrome*. London and Philadelphia: Jessica Kingsley Publishers.

Dubin, N. (2006) *Asperger Syndrome and Employment: A Personal Guide to Succeeding at Work (DVD)*. London and Philadelphia: Jessica Kingsley Publishers.

Edmonds, G. and Beardon, L. (2008) *Asperger Syndrome and Employment: Adults Speak Out About Asperger Syndrome*. London and Philadelphia: Jessica Kingsley Publishers.

Fast, Y. (2004) *Employment for Individuals with Asperger Syndrome or Non-Verbal Learning Disabilities: Stories and Strategies*. London and Philadelphia: Jessica Kingsley Publishers.

Grandin, T. and Duffy, K. (2008) *Developing Talents: Careers for Individuals with Asperger Syndrome and High-Functioning Autism*. Expanded Edition. Overland Park, KS: Autism Asperger Publishing Company.

Hawkins, G. (2003) *How to Find Work that Works for People with Asperger Syndrome: The Ultimate Guide for Getting People with Asperger Syndrome into the Workplace (and Keeping Them There!)*. London and Philadelphia: Jessica Kingsley Publishers.

Hendrickx, S. (2008) *Asperger Syndrome and Employment: What People with Asperger Syndrome Really Really Want*. London and Philadelphia: Jessica Kingsley Publishers.

Leach, S. (2002) *A Supported Employment Workbook: Using Individual Profiling and Job Matching*. London and Philadelphia: Jessica Kingsley Publishers.

Meyer, R.N. (2000) *Asperger Syndrome Employment Workbook: An Employment Workbook for Adults with Asperger Syndrome*. London and Philadelphia: Jessica Kingsley Publishers.

Simone, R. (2010) *Asperger's on the Job: Must-Have Advice for People with Asperger's of High Functioning Autism, and their Employers, Educators, and Advocates*. Arlington, TX: Future Horizons.

If you are seeking a position in management

Johnson, M. (2004) *Managing with Asperger Syndrome: A Practical Guide For White Collar Professionals*. London and Philadelphia: Jessica Kingsley Publishers.

If you are younger and just beginning work

Clements, J., Hardy, J., and Lord, S. (2010) *Transition or Transformation? Helping Young People with Autistic Spectrum Disorder Set Out on a Hopeful Road Towards Their Adult Lives.* London and Philadelphia: Jessica Kingsley Publishers.

About the Author

Ashley Stanford is the CEO of a computer company in California, USA. She also sits on the board of a non-profit company providing technical assistance on an international level to people who most need technical assistance.

Ashley's husband and eldest son both have Asperger Syndrome. Her second son also has AS and was a tremendous support and meticulous editor while Ashley wrote both this book and her previous book, *Asperger Syndrome and Long-Term Relationships*. Ashley's third son, Stephen, was diagnosed early with high-functioning autism "or possibly hyperlexia," but received such intense early intervention the traits are no longer visible during observation. (See the book *When Babies Read* by Audra Jensen, 2005, if you also have a child who reads early and has been identified as possibly autistic.) Ashley's last child, Suzetta, was found to be "...probably on the spectrum, but she's such a *girl*..." Diagnoses are tricky things.

Question: Why hide behind a pen name again?

Answer: Because privacy helps me survive the intense pressures of an overscheduled life.

With this book, I need the pen name because my professional life is bubbling over with too much responsibility. For my previous book, *Asperger Syndrome and Long-Term Relationships* I needed the pen name because my personal life was not just bubbling, but erupting with responsibilities that were more than I could handle. While pregnant with my fourth and final child, my doctor ordered me on bed-rest.

For several months I was confined to bed. I pulled out my trusty laptop and did the best I could to stay calm.

My youngest recently had been diagnosed with either high-functioning autism or AS or hyperlexia depending on which professional I asked. Also, during this time of tumultuous "rest," my husband opened up to the possibility that his unique traits were all explainable through the AS diagnosis.

We were traveling a path that is probably familiar to you, dear reader. We were exploring the AS diagnosis and seeing with brutal clarity how it had shaped our lives for better and for worse. It is unfortunate that, in hindsight, it was too easy to see how the nexus, the starting point of each of our arguments, had been couched in the specifics of the AS diagnostic criteria. Fortunately, the diagnosis explained so much that, despite the regret, it felt much like opening a new window and letting in the fresh air.

During these months of bed-rest, I dove deep into researching AS. I now had a little baby boy who actively avoided eye contact and had panic attacks related to the sensory stimuli in the environment. Even as a newborn learning to control the movements of his own head, he struggled to avoid faces looking at him. As he was learning to walk, he was tippy toe, walking like a ballerino (male ballerina). With a bit of fear, I worried that my final child, still in my belly, might or might not need assistance on the all-consuming level her brother did.

I researched Asperger Syndrome with a vengeance and the result was *Asperger Syndrome and Long-Term Relationships*, published by Jessica Kingsley Publishers, my number one choice for publisher. I will never forget the day after my daughter's birth, when I reread the first print copy with my baby girl sleeping in my arms and tears pouring down my cheeks because of the overpowering, intoxicating combination of gratitude and complete fear. The gratitude, because I had found a resource (a publisher) that would give voice to what I had created, and the fear, because I was now aware of the urgent time-sensitive needs of my son and also of the permanence of my husband's neural structure.

I chose to use a pen name for the first book because the weight of my responsibilities at that point in my life was so heavy and so all-encompassing that I could not allow any other input in my life. The publisher forwarded letters, but beyond that I was completely unavailable. I was in Mother Bear Protective mode (known in our home as MBP).

Many of you may have gone through similar phases of life where you have had no other goal than self-protection.

I felt an appropriately intense desire to protect my family, especially considering what I knew now of my husband and son's internal experience. My husband had been trying so hard, too hard to "pretend to be normal," a term coined by Liane Holliday Willey that encompassed so well the many AS coping mechanisms my husband had developed. It was Liane Holliday Willey's book and Tony Attwood's book on AS that were our gentle and much appreciated initial entry into this healing phase of our lives (Attwood 2008; Holliday Willey 1999).

Now, eight years later, I am again opting for a pen name although for a more personally selfish reason. As I have grown professionally, I have built yet another time-intensive lifestyle. I use a pen name again in order to keep my own load manageable and to keep the family happily under their shield of anonymity.

If you also have Asperger Syndrome, you can probably relate to the desire to be private, to make the world go away from time to time. Privacy and solitude are highly prized possessions. They can be survival tools in a chaotic world.

Note that I give the same respect to the people I quote in this book. All names have been changed except those names of published authors and researchers.

As my daughter once said when she was in preschool: "I wish I was a turtle. Then I could hide whenever I wanted." Thank you for granting me the right to hide when I published my first book. My most heartfelt thanks go out to you again as I publish my second: thank you for allowing me to keep my beloved turtle shell. It gives me a deeply comforting sense of safety.

The purpose of this book is to help you find the same sense of safety and personal comfort as you build and shape your own career.

Index